DIABETIC DIET AFTER 50

1500 Days of Tasty Low-Carbs Recipes with a 30-Day Meal Plan for People Over 50 to Live a Low-Sugar Healthy Lifestyle

Angelica Haig

Table of Contents

Introduction

If you are newly diagnosed with type 2 diabetes, it can be an overwhelming experience. You may feel lost and unsure of how to proceed with your dietary choices. However, with the new ***DIABETIC DIET AFTER 50***, you can transform that challenge into a delicious opportunity. With across 1500 days' worth of tasty and quick recipes, this cookbook provides a month-long meal plan to ease you smoothly into a new, healthier way of life. We aim to make it easy for you to make the necessary changes in your life without sacrificing taste or variety.

The book starts with an introduction to the main changes our body experiences after 50s, it goes then to explain diabetes and provides essential information on understanding its root causes, symptoms, different types of diabetes, and prediabetes condition. We've also included a section on healthy lifestyle habits that will help you combat diabetes and enhance your overall well-being, specially focused on habits for people over 50. With the foundations laid, the cookbook cover a wide range of recipes, including breakfast, main dishes, snacks, desserts, and everything in among - all designed to be diabetic-friendly without skimping on flavor. In addition, we have ensured that the ingredients needed for each recipe are readily available, so even someone with limited cooking experience can create healthy and delicious meals.

Each recipe highlights key nutritional information such as calories, carbohydrates, fats, proteins, and sugar so that you can make informed decisions for planning guilt-free and wholesome meals. Additionally, we've gone one step further by offering a comprehensive 30-day meal plan to ease you into this new way of eating. You'll find meticulously planned daily menus consisting of well-balanced meals and enticing treats - because adopting a healthy lifestyle should not be synonymous with deprivation.

As you indulge in the culinary delights of this cookbook and experience firsthand the benefits of a healthy, balanced diet, we hope to inspire you to embrace a transformative and vibrant lifestyle that supports your well-being. So, don't wait any longer – embark on this life-changing journey today!

We used some icons to make your reading experience more fun:

 Preparation Time

 Cooking Time

 Servings

Chapter 1: How Your Body Changes After 50

Growing older can be especially challenging for those with diabetes or at risk of developing it, as our bodies undergo a variety of changes that can make managing the condition more complex. Hence, it's crucial to understand how our bodies change after 50, particularly if we're already managing diabetes or pre-diabetes. In this comprehensive section, we will discuss key body changes after 5 decades of life, plus effective strategies for addressing any difficulties that may arise in managing diabetes after 50.

1. Age-Related Slowing of Metabolism- One significant transformation that occurs after 50 is the slowing down of metabolism. The decline in metabolism can lead to weight gain and make the management of blood sugar levels increasingly tough for those with diabetes. Incorporating a well-balanced diet can help mitigate this age-related issue - opt for whole foods rich in dietary fiber, healthy fats, and lean protein sources.

2. Decreased Insulin Sensitivity- Insulin resistance increases with age, heightening the risk of developing Type 2 diabetes if you haven't been diagnosed yet. Moderate exercise is an excellent solution to increase insulin sensitivity, helping your body to better utilize glucose from the bloodstream.

3. Loss of Lean Muscle Mass- As we age, it's natural to lose muscle mass due to lowered testosterone levels and decreased physical activity levels. Muscle tissue plays a pivotal role in your body's ability to utilize glucose effectively; hence, losing muscle increases the challenge in managing glucose levels. Strength-training exercises are essential for regaining and maintaining lean muscle mass while enhancing glucose regulation.

4. Changes in Hormone Levels- Giving special attention to hormonal changes after turning 50 is imperative for both men and women since fluctuations can impact blood sugar levels directly or indirectly when living with diabetes. For instance, post-menopausal women might experience elevated insulin resistance due to dropping estrogen levels. Additionally, men with low testosterone levels are at an increased risk of developing insulin resistance. Consult your doctor if you believe hormonal changes are affecting your blood sugar control.

5. Medication Changes and Interactions- You may be prescribed new medications as you age, which can interfere with your diabetes management. Some drugs may instigate glucose fluctuations or interact with your diabetic treatment plan. Communicate openly with your healthcare provider about any changes in your medication routine and consistently monitor blood sugar levels to ensure optimal management.

6. Changes in Kidney Function- Our kidney function can decline as we age, which is crucial to bear in mind if you're living with diabetes. This can impact the clearance of medications or insulin from our body, and potentially lead to episodes of hypoglycemia or hyperglycemia. Regular appointments with your healthcare provider can help detect changes in kidney functioning early on and aid in adapting your treatment plan.

7. Cognitive Function- With aging, cognitive decline is a possibility, making diabetes management slightly more challenging. This underscores the importance of creating simplified and structured routines for medication administration, monitoring blood sugar levels, and meal planning.

Additionally, discuss concerns about cognitive decline with your healthcare provider who can provide guidance on managing diabetes effectively.

As aging brings forth numerous challenges for those diagnosed with or at risk of diabetes, being aware of the changes our bodies undergo and how they impact diabetes management is crucial. Staying proactive in implementing healthy habits like regular exercise, mindful eating, frequent check-ups with your healthcare provider, and self-monitoring blood sugar levels will empower you to maintain better control of your diabetes after turning 50.

Remember that lifestyle modifications play a significant role in maintaining good overall health and wellbeing while coping with diabetes. If required, seek support from family members or engage the services of a dietician or certified diabetic educator to help guide you through adapting new healthy habits into your daily life smoothly.

Chapter 2: Understanding Diabetes

Studying diabetes in detail is crucial in managing the condition and maintaining a healthy lifestyle. Diabetes is a metabolic illness that impairs either the capacity of the body to create insulin or its capacity to make good implement of the insulin it already has, leading to increased levels of sugar in the blood. Several risk factors contribute to developing diabetes, such as genetics, obesity, a sedentary lifestyle, and poor diet. Symptoms might consist of recurrent urination, increased thirst, unexplained weight loss, blurry vision, and tiredness. It is essential to diagnose and treat diabetes early to avoid problems such as heart disease, stroke, kidney damage, and vision problems.

To manage diabetes, individuals must monitor and control their blood sugar levels through medication, healthy eating, regular physical activity, and stress management. This may involve taking insulin injections or oral medications and following a balanced diet focusing on complex carbohydrates and fiber-rich foods while limiting refined sugars and unhealthy fats.

In addition to medical treatments, self-care plays a vital role in managing diabetes. Regular monitoring of blood pressure and cholesterol levels reduces risk factors for cardiovascular diseases. Understanding the impact of various factors like emotional stress and illness on blood sugar fluctuations helps people with diabetes make informed decisions about their daily routines.

Education about diabetes management and collaboration with healthcare professionals enhance one's quality of life while living with this chronic condition.

Types of Diabetes and Prediabetes Explained

In this section, we'll explore the various kinds of diabetes and look closely at prediabetes - a lesser-known but equally important condition.

1. Type 1 Diabetes- Insulin-producing cells in the pancreas are targeted by the immune system of a person with type 1 diabetes, and this ends in their death. Type 1 diabetes is an autoimmune illness, causing glucose to accumulate in the blood. Approximately 6 to 12 % of people with diabetes have type 1 diabetes. It generally starts in childhood or early adulthood and needs daily insulin injections for survival.

2. Type 2 Diabetes- The vast majority of people who are diagnosed with diabetes have type 2, making up around 80 to 90 % of every instance globally. In this situation, the cells of the body either grow immune to the effects of insulin or fail to generate sufficient insulin to satisfy the requirements of the body. Although lifestyle factors such as obesity, a poor diet, and an absence of physical activity are frequently linked to type 2 diabetes, genetics could also have a role in the development of the condition. It can be managed through lifestyle modifications such as regular exercise, healthy eating habits, and weight control.

3. Gestational Diabetes- Diabetes mellitus, often known as gestational diabetes or simply diabetes, is a kind of the disease that only affects pregnant women who didn't suffer from diabetes prior to becoming pregnant. It occurs when the insulin-regulating hormones produced by the placenta start to malfunction, leading to higher blood sugar levels. Although gestational diabetes can generally be managed through diet and exercise, it can surge the risk of complications during pregnancy and delivery, like preeclampsia, cesarean delivery, and neonatal hypoglycemia. Those diagnosed with gestational diabetes should be monitored closely by their healthcare providers to prevent future health problems.

4. Prediabetes- A condition known as prediabetes occurs when a person has high blood sugar levels whereas they aren't quite sufficiently elevated to be diagnosed with diabetes. It's an important warning sign that allows individuals to take preventive measures to avoid developing type 2 diabetes. There are usually no obvious symptoms of prediabetes, making it crucial for individuals with risk factors like obesity, a family history of diabetes, or a sedentary lifestyle to get tested regularly.

Lifestyle modifications like healthy eating habits, weight loss, and amplified physical activity can help delay or avert the progression from prediabetes to type 2 diabetes.

Understanding the various kinds of diabetes and prediabetes plays a vital role in managing personal health. Knowing the early warning signs can help individuals seek medical intervention promptly, reducing complications associated with untreated diabetes. Adopting a healthier lifestyle can go a long way in preventing or managing this chronic condition.

Chapter 3: How Your Metabolism Change After 50

One of the most notable changes that occur after turning 50 is the alteration in our metabolism. Often, people notice a gradual weight gain, an increase in fatigue, and shifts in their hormones. Here, we will explore how and why your metabolism changes after the age of 50, as well as some strategies to help you maintain a healthy metabolism as you age.

The Metabolic Process

Metabolism is the complex chemical process by which our bodies convert the food we consume into energy. It plays a crucial role in various bodily functions such as growth, repair, and maintenance of cells. Our basal metabolic rate (BMR)—the amount of energy our bodies burn while at rest—plays a substantial role in determining how effectively our metabolisms work.

Factors Contributing to Metabolic Changes After 50

1. Age-related muscle loss: As we age, it's natural for our bodies to lose muscle mass—a phenomenon known as sarcopenia. Since muscle tissue burns more calories than fat tissue, losing muscle mass leads to a slower metabolism. Research shows that adults can lose three to five percent of their muscle mass per decade after turning thirty, with the rate increasing with age.

2. Hormonal changes: Around the age of 50, many individuals undergo significant hormonal shifts. For women experiencing menopause, estrogen levels drop and can contribute to weight gain and reduced energy levels. For men entering andropause, testosterone levels decrease which can lead to fatigue and a slower metabolism.

3. Reduction in physical activity: As we grow older, we may become less physically active due to various factors such as joint pain or decreased mobility – this contributes to slower metabolism rates along with decreased muscle mass and weight gain.

4. Reduced Basal Metabolic Rate (BMR): With age, our BMR drops because both muscle mass and the rate at which our bodies burn calories decrease significantly. This can make it more challenging to maintain our weight or shed extra pounds.

Strategies for Boosting Metabolism After 50

1. Strength training: Resistance exercises focusing on building and strengthening muscles are essential to stave off age-related muscle loss. Aim for at least two strength training sessions per week, targeting major muscle groups.

2. Engaging in regular aerobic exercise: Incorporating activities such as walking, jogging, swimming, or cycling can help maintain a healthy weight and support your metabolism while also promoting cardiovascular health.

3. Consuming a balanced diet: Ensure that your diet includes plenty of high-quality protein sources like lean meats, legumes, nuts, and dairy to support muscle growth and maintenance. Additionally, opt for whole grains, fruits, vegetables, and healthy fats to provide energy and promote overall health.

4. Prioritizing sleep: Our bodies require adequate restorative sleep for various functions including hormone regulation, cognitive processes, and cell repair. Aim for seven to nine hours of quality sleep each night to avoid negatively affecting your metabolism.

5. *Moderating stress levels:* Elevated stress levels can wreak havoc on your hormones and impact your metabolic rate. Incorporate stress management techniques such as meditation, deep breathing exercises, or yoga into your daily routine to help mitigate the impact of stress on your metabolism.

6. *Staying hydrated:* Drinking water is vital for overall health because it aids digestion and is necessary for the proper functioning of all bodily processes, including metabolism. Make sure you are drinking enough water throughout the day by carrying a reusable bottle with you or setting reminders to take water breaks.

While it's natural for our metabolisms to change as we age, various strategies can help us maintain a healthy metabolic rate after hitting the big 5-0. By focusing on a balanced diet, prioritizing physical activity with an emphasis on strength training, and maintaining a healthy lifestyle, we can help counteract the effects of age-related metabolic changes and continue enjoying vibrant health even after the age of 50.

Chapter 4: How To Prevent Diabetes After 50

As we age, the risk of developing this health condition increases, particularly after the age of 50. In this comprehensive blog post, we will explore how to prevent diabetes after 50 by covering various aspects such as understanding diabetes, the importance of a healthy lifestyle, and actionable steps for prevention.

Understanding Diabetes

To fully understand diabetes, we need to learn its main types. The first one (Type one) is where the body mistakenly destroys pancreatic beta cells, halting insulin production. Without insulin, glucose cannot enter cells, leading to increase of blood sugar levels. The symptoms include often urination, increased thirst, hunger, and fatigue. It mainly affects children and young adults but can occur at any age. Management includes regular blood sugar monitoring, insulin therapy, and maintaining a balanced diet and exercise. Despite its challenges, people with Type 1 Diabetes can lead fulfilling lives through effective care and management.

On the other hand, diabetes type two is the most common and accounts for about ninety percent of all cases. It occurs when the body becomes resistant to insulin, resulting in high blood sugar levels. Risk factors include obesity, poor diet, and a sedentary lifestyle. Common symptoms include increased thirst and urination, fatigue, and blurred vision. Management involves lifestyle changes like healthy eating, active exercise, and healthy weight. Medications and insulin therapy may also be prescribed for controlling blood sugar levels. Early diagnosis plus treatment is crucial to avoid further complications.

Both types are characterized by high blood sugar levels, which can lead to many other complications if not control correctly. After the age of 50, individuals become more susceptible to developing Type 2 diabetes due to natural physiological changes and lifestyle factors. Having a deeper understanding of this condition will enable us to make informed decisions about our health and lifestyle choices.

Importance of a Healthy Lifestyle

A healthy lifestyle is crucial in preventing diabetes, especially after the age of 50 when there is an increased risk. The following are essential components of maintaining a healthy lifestyle:

1. Diet: A well-balanced diet is vital for managing blood sugar levels and overall health. Consuming more fruits, vegetables, lean protein sources, whole grains, and reducing refined sugars can significantly lower your risk for diabetes.

2. Exercise: It can help for blood sugar regulation, insulin sensitivity improvement, and lessen possible diabetes type two development after the age of 50. Exercise daily, aim to get one hundred fifty mins of moderate exercise weekly, and engage in resistance training at least twice a week as you age.

3. Sleep: Adequate sleep is vital for overall well-being and hormonal balance. Poor sleep can disrupt hormones that regulate blood sugar levels, thus increasing the risk for diabetes.

4. Stress Management: Chronic stress elevates cortisol levels, which can contribute to high blood sugar and diabetes risk. Simple lifestyle modifications like practicing meditation or yoga, engaging in hobbies that reduce stress, and maintaining healthy relationships can aid in stress reduction.

5. *Regular Health Check-ups:* Visit your doctor for regular medical check-ups to monitor glucose levels, blood pressure, plus cholesterol. Early diagnosis and treatment can prevent complications of diabetes.

Actionable Steps for Prevention

Preventing diabetes after 50 revolves around integrating these healthy lifestyle measures and setting realistic goals. The following actionable steps will help you take charge of your health:

1. *Adopt Nutrient-dense Diet:* Fill your plate with an array of colorful vegetables and fruits, lean protein sources, whole grains, plus healthy fats.

2. *Limit Refined Sugars and Processed Foods:* Avoid foods high in refined sugars like candy, soda, cookies, and processed carbohydrates such as white bread or pasta.

3. *Get Active:* Aim for regular physical activity by incorporating activities you enjoy, such as walking, gardening or swimming. Start small and gradually increase the duration and intensity of exercise.

4. *Maintain a Healthy Weight:* A healthy weight reduces the risk for diabetes along with other health problems. Seek guidance from a healthcare professional if you need help losing weight.

5. *Quit Smoking:* It increases the development of diabetes type two as it restricts blood flow and impairs insulin production.

6. *Alcohol Consumption:* Alcohol intake affects your blood sugar levels and may play a role in weight gain. Excessive drinking also increases the risk of developing certain conditions like pancreatitis, which can lead to the onset of diabetes. If you drink, do so moderately and never on an empty stomach.

7. *Prioritize Mental Health:* Reducing stress is an essential step in managing blood sugars. Identify the sources of stress in your life and find appropriate coping strategies like mindfulness or seeking professional help if needed.

8. *Keep Learning:* Stay informed about new research on diabetes prevention by reading articles published in medical journals, attending conferences, or webinars hosted by reputable sources.

Preventing diabetes after 50 is a combination of understanding the condition, adopting a healthy lifestyle, and committing to making better choices throughout your life. By following the necessary precautions and being proactive in your approach, you can successfully lessen possible diabetes development and live a healthy, fulfilling life. Remember that it's never too late to start taking control of your health.

Chapter 5: Healthy Alternatives to Replace Sugar

Living with diabetes requires being mindful of your sugar intake, but that doesn't mean you have to eliminate sweetness from your diet completely. Several healthy alternatives to sugar can help manage blood sugar levels while still providing the sweetness you crave.

1. Stevia: Derived from the leaves of the Stevia rebaudiana plant, stevia is a natural sweetener with zero calories and no effect on blood sugar levels. It's available in liquid, granulated, and powdered forms, making it an easy recipe swap for sugar.

2. Erythritol: A sugar alcohol, erythritol has 70% of the sweetness of sugar with only 5% of the calories. It's a low-glycemic sweetener that won't spike blood sugar levels, making it an ideal choice for those with diabetes.

3. Xylitol: Another sugar alcohol, xylitol, has the same sweetness as sugar but with 40% fewer calories. It has a low glycemic index and may even help prevent tooth decay. However, it's important to note that xylitol can be toxic to dogs, so keep it away from pets.

4. Monk Fruit Sweetener: Extracted from monk fruit, this natural sweetener is calorie-free and does not affect blood sugar levels. It's available in liquid or powder form and can be used to replace sugar in cooking and baking.

5. Yacon Syrup: Made from the yacon plant's roots, this syrup contains fructooligosaccharides (FOS) – a natural sweetener that does not increase blood glucose levels as it passes through your system undigested. Yacon syrup can be used as a drizzle on yogurt or oatmeal or in place of honey in certain recipes.

While these alternatives are healthier for people with diabetes, consuming them in moderation is important.

Chapter 6: Effective Meal Planning for a Dynamic and Less Frustrating Diet

Planning meals ahead of time can help make this process less frustrating and more dynamic. Here are some steps to plan your meals effectively:

1. Determine your nutritional needs: Consult with a dietitian or healthcare professional to establish the appropriate balance of carbohydrates, proteins, and fats for your specific needs. This will help you create a meal plan that supports healthy blood sugar levels while satisfying your dietary requirements.

2. Plan a diverse menu: Include a diversity of foods from all food groups to keep your diet exciting and ensure you're getting all the necessary nutrients. Incorporate lean proteins, whole grains, fruits, vegetables, and healthy fats in your meal planning.

3. Use meal planning tools: Consider utilizing smartphone apps or websites designed for diabetics to plan your meals ahead of time. Alternatively, you can create your own meal planner or use a calendar to map out your weekly meals.

4. Prepare meals in advance: Cook big batches of food on the weekends or on days when you have more time to spare. Store these meals in portions in the refrigerator or freezer to easily heat them up during busier weekdays.

5. Keep snacks on hand: Always have healthy snacks available for among-meal munching or when you need an energy boost. Options like fresh fruits, nuts, seeds, and low-fat yogurt are great choices.

6. Monitor portion sizes: Ensure that you are serving yourself appropriate portions of each food group based on your diabetic meal plan. Overeating can lead to elevated blood sugar levels and weight gain.

7. Stay flexible: Give yourself room to adjust your meal plan as needed. If you find a certain food is causing a spike in your blood sugar, swap it out for a better option. Track how different meals impact your blood sugar levels to find the best balance.

8. Find support: Connect with friends, family members, or support groups who also have diabetes or are focused on healthy eating habits. Sharing recipes, meal plans, and experiences can make the process less daunting and more enjoyable.

Chapter 7: Breakfast Recipes

Spinach Shakshuka

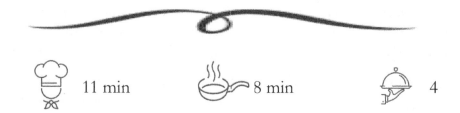

11 min   8 min   4

Ingredients:

- a jar of no-sugar marinara sauce, such as Rao's
- ¼ cup extra-virgin olive oil
- 6 ½ oz spinach, thawed & drained of excess liquid
- 4 big eggs
- 5 ounces shredded mozzarella cheese

Directions:

1. Inside a deep skillet with a lid, combine the marinara sauce, olive oil, spinach, and stir till thoroughly mixed.
2. Let the mixture boil at moderate-high flame, afterwards adjust to low heat, cover, and boil for a couple of minutes.
3. Uncover the skillet and gently crack each egg into the simmering sauce, allowing the egg to create a crater and being careful not to let the eggs touch. Return the lid and cook within eight to ten mins, poaching the eggs till the yolks are set.
4. Uncover and scatter with the cheese. Return the cover and cook within three to five mins till cheese is melted and the eggs are fully cooked. Serve warm.

Nutritional Values:

- Calories: 395
- Net Carbs: 9g
- Fat: 32g
- Protein: 17g
- Sugar: 0g

Difficulty: 1 **2** 3 4 5

Apple Cinnamon Scones

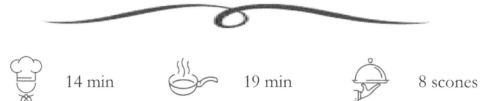

14 min   19 min   8 scones

Ingredients:

- one and a half cups almond flour
- half cup coconut flour
- quarter cup granulated erythritol
- one and a half teaspoons baking powder
- one tsp. ground cinnamon
- quarter tsp. salt
- quarter cup unsweetened applesauce
- one big egg, lightly beaten
- quarter cup unsweetened almond milk
- three tbsp coconut oil, dissolved & cooled slightly
- one tsp vanilla extract
- one average apple, skinned & thinly diced

Directions:

1. Warm up the oven to 350°F. Line a baking tray utilizing parchment paper.
2. Whisk together the almond flour, coconut flour, erythritol, baking powder, cinnamon, and salt in your big container.
3. Combine all together the applesauce, beaten egg, almond milk, melted coconut oil, and vanilla extract in a different bowl.
4. Merge the wet and dry mixtures. Fold in the diced apple pieces utilizing a spatula. Shape your dough into a ball and put it on your baking tray.
5. Level the dough into 8" circle about an inch thick. Cut the dough into eight equal wedges but don't separate them yet.
6. Bake within 20 mins till lightly golden. Cool it down, carefully separate the scones, then serve.

Nutritional Values:

- Calories: 220
- Net Carbs: 5g
- Fat: 17g
- Protein: 7g
- Sugar: 3g

Difficulty: 1 2 **3** 4 5

Avocado Toast with Fried Egg

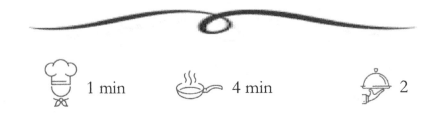

1 min   4 min   2

Ingredients:

- two low-carb bread toasted slices
- 1 medium ripe avocado, peeled and finely sliced
- 1 tbsp + 2 tsp extra-virgin olive oil
- 2 big eggs
- ½ teaspoon ground black pepper

Directions:

1. Arrange the avocado slices on the toasted bread slices.
2. Warm 1 tbsp olive oil inside a moderate nonstick skillet across moderate-high flame. Cook the eggs for 1 to 2 mins per side.
3. Place 1 fried egg atop the avocado slices on every bread slice. Sprinkle each with little pepper and drizzle one tsp. of olive oil. Serve warm.

Nutritional Values:

- Calories: 451
- Net Carbs: 3g
- Fat: 42g
- Protein: 13g
- Sugar: 0g

Difficulty: **1** 2 3 4 5

Poppyseed Lemon Muffins

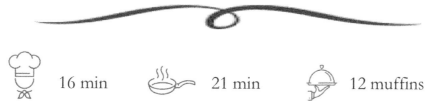

16 min   21 min   12 muffins

Ingredients:

- ½ cup extra-virgin olive oil
- half cup sour cream
- 3 big eggs
- one teaspoon vanilla extract
- 1 lemon zest

- ½ cup granulated sugar-free sweetener, such as Swerve
- 1¾ cups almond flour
- one and a half tsps. baking powder
- one teaspoon xanthan gum (optional)
- one and a half tsp poppyseeds

Directions:

1. Warm up the oven to 350°F. Line a twelve-cup muffin tin utilizing liners.
2. Toss simultaneously the olive oil, sour cream, eggs, vanilla, lemon zest, and granulated sweetener inside your big container.
3. Include the almond flour, baking powder, xanthan gum (if utilizing), and poppyseeds, and mix till well incorporated.
4. Split the batter uniformly amongst your muffin cups, topping all about ¾ complete. Bake within 16 to 18 mins till golden.

Nutritional Values:

- Calories: 215
- Net Carbs: 2g
- Fat: 21g
- Protein: 5g
- Sugar: 8g

Difficulty: 1 2 **3** 4 5

Blueberry French Toast

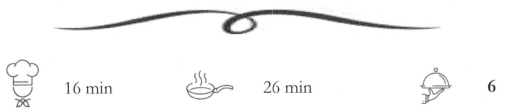

🍳 16 min   🍳 26 min   🍽 6

Ingredients:

- 12 chopped low-carb bread
- 6 big eggs
- one cup almond milk (unsweetened)
- one tsp vanilla extract
- ½ teaspoon cinnamon
- two cups fresh or frozen blueberries
- sugar-free maple syrup for serving (not mandatory)

Directions:

1. Warm up oven to 350°F. Slightly oil your baking tray.
2. Arrange the low-carb bread slices in your baking dish, slightly overlapping.
3. Whisk together eggs, unsweetened almond milk, vanilla extract, and cinnamon in your bowl. Pour your egg mixture evenly across the bread slices.
4. Scatter the blueberries across the soaked bread. Bake within 25 mins till the surface is slightly brown and the center is set.
5. Take it out and allow it to cool for a couple of mins before cutting it into servings. Serve with sugar-free maple syrup if you like.

Nutritional Values:

- Calories: 215
- Net Carbs: 7g
- Fat: 12g
- Protein: 15g
- Sugar: 3g

Difficulty: 1 **2** 3 4 5

Baked Oatmeal with Berries

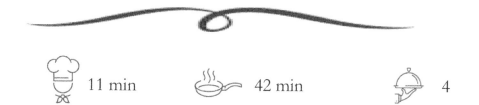

11 min   42 min   4

Ingredients:

- one tbsp coconut oil or cooking spray
- one cup unsweetened almond milk
- half cup hemp hearts
- 1 tsp cinnamon
- one teaspoon vanilla extract
- four big eggs

- ¼ cup ground flaxseed
- one teaspoon baking powder
- ½ cup berries (such as blueberries, raspberries, blackberries, or chopped strawberries)

Directions:

1. Warm up the oven to 375°F. Oil an eight inch loaf pot utilizing coconut oil or cooking spray.
2. In your small pot on high flame, let the milk boil. Include hemp hearts, then adjust to low heat and simmer within eight-ten mins, often stirring, till thickened. Remove and stir in cinnamon and vanilla.
3. Toss simultaneously the eggs, flaxseed, and baking powder in your big container. Include in the warm hemp mixture, whisking constantly. Mix in the berries and transfer the solution to your loaf pan.
4. Bake for twenty to twenty-five mins, till fully set. Take out and cool it down before slicing. Serve.

Nutritional Values:

- Calories: 278
- Net Carbs: 6g
- Fat: 22g
- Protein: 15g
- Sugar: 0g

Difficulty: 1 **2** 3 4 5

Whipped Cottage Cheese Bowl

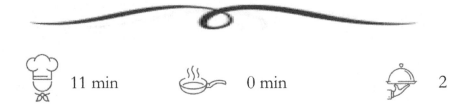

🧑‍🍳 11 min   🍳 0 min   🍽 2

Ingredients:

- one cup full-fat cottage cheese
- half cup heavy whipping cream
- quarter cup chopped walnuts
- quarter cup unsweetened shredded coconut
- quarter cup fresh blueberries
- one tsp vanilla extract
- keto-friendly Sweetener of choice to taste
- Pinch of cinnamon (optional)

Directions:

1. Put the cottage cheese and heavy cream into a mixer. Mix till smooth. Taste for sweetness, and include keto-friendly sweetener if desired.
2. Divide the whipped cottage cheese mixture equally into two containers. Top each container with 1/2 walnuts, coconut, and blueberries.
3. Drizzle with vanilla and cinnamon, if desired. Serve.

Nutritional Values:

- Calories: 450
- Net Carbs: 8g
- Fat: 40g
- Protein: 15g
- Sugar: 5g

Difficulty: **1** 2 3 4 5

Almond Butter Pancakes

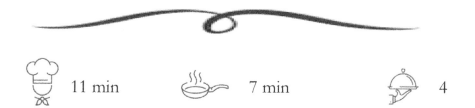

🧑‍🍳 11 min   🍳 7 min   🍽 4

Ingredients:

- half cup creamy unsweetened almond butter
- 2 big eggs
- ½ cup unsweetened almond milk, + more as needed
- one cup almond flour
- one tsp. baking powder
- Cooking spray, coconut oil, or butter

Directions:

1. Whisk together the almond butter, eggs, and almond milk in your container till uniform and creamy.
2. Mix in almond flour plus baking powder till uniform. If the batter is dense, include almond milk 1 tbsp at a time till pourable.
3. Heat your big nonstick griddle on moderate-low flame and spray or drizzle oil. Put ¼ cup of batter and cook for 4-5 mins, till the edges begin to firm up.
4. Flip and cook within a couple of minutes. Replicate with the remaining batter. Serve warm.

Nutritional Values:

- Calories: 396
- Net Carbs: 6g
- Fat: 34g
- Protein: 16g
- Sugar: 0g

Difficulty: 1 2 **3** 4 5

Berry Walnut Yoghurt Parfait

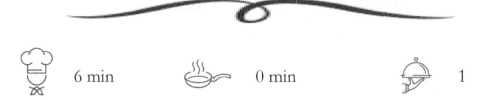

🧑‍🍳 6 min   🍳 0 min   🍽 1

Ingredients:

- half cup plain whole-milk (4 or 5 % milk fat) Greek yogurt
- one tablespoon unsweetened almond or peanut butter
- ½ tsp vanilla extract (optional)
- ½ tsp cinnamon (optional)
- 2 tbsp chopped walnuts
- ¼ cup fresh berries

Directions:

1. Inside a serving container, whisk the yogurt, almond butter, vanilla (if using), and cinnamon (if using).
2. Top with the chopped nuts and berries, and serve immediately.

Nutritional Values:

- Calories: 316
- Net Carbs: 10g
- Fat: 23g
- Protein: 17g
- Sugar: 0g

Difficulty: **1** 2 3 4 5

Sausage and Cheese Egg Muffin

11 min   23 min   4

Ingredients:

- Nonstick cooking spray
- ½ pound breakfast sausage, casings removed
- 8 big eggs
- half cup shredded Cheddar cheese
- quarter cup sliced scallions, both white and green shares
- ¼ tsp. kosher salt
- quarter tsp. ground black pepper

Directions:

1. Warm up your oven to 350°F. Mildly spray 6 cups of a regular-size muffin can with cooking spray.
2. Cook the breakfast sausage within 6 mins till no pink remains. Drain any fat.
3. Whip the eggs with a fork or a whisk inside a moderate container till frothy and thoroughly combined. Include the cooked sausage, cheese, scallions, salt, and pepper to the eggs. Combine thoroughly.
4. Split the egg and sausage mixture among the 6 muffin cups and bake for 15 to 17 mins or till set within the middle.

Nutritional Values:

- Calories: 399
- Net Carbs: 2g
- Fat: 32g
- Protein: 24g
- Sugar: 0g

Difficulty: 1 **2** 3 4 5

Eggs Stuffed Avocado Boats

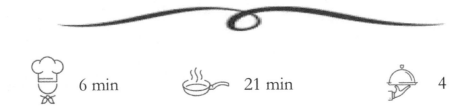

6 min   21 min   4

Ingredients:

- two ripe avocados, cut in half lengthwise & pitted
- four big eggs
- Kosher salt & ground black pepper, as required
- four slices bacon, cooked & sliced

Directions:

1. Warm up the oven to 350 degrees F.
2. Use your spatula to scoop out the avocado flesh to make the pit hollow bigger, big enough to hold the egg. Crack an egg into the scooped-out hole of each avocado half.
3. Drizzle the avocado halves utilizing salt & pepper and put them onto a baking tray. Bake for 20 mins till the eggs are set.
4. Garnish the cooked avocado boats with the crispy bacon and serve.

Nutritional Values:

- Calories: 289
- Net Carbs: 2g
- Fat: 24g
- Protein: 12g
- Sugar: 0g

Difficulty: 1 2 **3** 4 5

Breakfast Potato Zucchini Hash

🧑‍🍳 16 min   🍳 17 min   🍽 4

Ingredients:

- ½ cup shredded yellow waxy potato
- 1½ cups shredded zucchini
- 1 tsp salt
- 1 pound ground Italian pork sausage
- ¼ cup extra-virgin olive oil
- one tsp. garlic powder (optional)
- ¼ tsp. grounded black pepper

Directions:

1. Mix the shredded potato and zucchini in a colander or on numerous layers of paper towels.
2. Drizzle with the salt and allow to sit for ten mins. Utilizing another paper towel, press on the vegetables to release any excess moisture.
3. Meanwhile, heat an average-deep griddle across moderate-high flame. Include the sausage and cook within 8-10 mins till browned and cooked through. Transmit it to a container, reserving the rendered fat in the pot.
4. Include olive oil to the rendered fat and heat across moderate-high flame. Include the drained potato and zucchini.
5. Drizzle utilizing the garlic powder (if utilizing) and pepper, and fry for two mins, without stirring. Utilizing a spatula, stir the vegetables in the oil, and start to fry for another two to three mins or till crispy and cooked.
6. Return the cooked sausage to the griddle and fry for additional 1-2 mins or till reheated. Serve warm.

Nutritional Values:

- Calories: 533
- Net Carbs: 16g
- Fat: 40g
- Protein: 23g
- Sugar: 0g

Difficulty: 1 2 3 **4** 5

Pesto Egg and Ham Roll-Ups

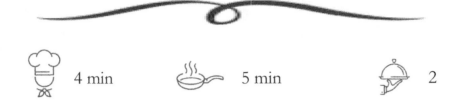

🧑‍🍳 4 min   🍳 5 min   🍽 2

Ingredients:

- four big eggs
- quarter cup jarred pesto (preferably made with olive oil)
- ½ tsp. salt
- quarter tsp. ground black pepper
- two tablespoon extra-virgin olive oil
- 4 big slices of thick-cut uncured ham or turkey

Directions:

1. Whisk simultaneously the eggs, pesto, salt, and pepper in your moderate container.
2. Warm the olive oil in your average griddle across moderate flame. Pour the egg solution, adjust to low heat, and cook within three-four mins, stirring frequently, till set. Eliminate.
3. Put the ham slices onto an oven-safe plate and oven on high for 15 secs or till heated through.
4. Place 1/4 egg mixture on each ham slice and roll like to secure like a burrito. Serve warm.

Nutritional Values:

- Calories: 537
- Net Carbs: 5g
- Fat: 40g
- Protein: 39g
- Sugar: 0g

Difficulty: 1 **2** 3 4 5

Corned Beef Hash

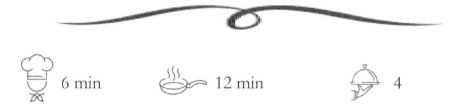

🍳 6 min   🍳 12 min   🍽 4

Ingredients:

- one tablespoon avocado oil
- one (12-oz) can of corned beef
- 1 cup radishes, cut into ¼-inch dice
- ¼ tsp garlic powder
- ¼ tsp ground black pepper

Directions:

1. Warm the oil in your big griddle across moderate-high flame till shimmering but not smoking. Include the corned beef and radishes, utilizing a spatula to break up the corned beef.
2. Cook across moderate flame within 8-10 mins, occasionally mixing, till the radishes are tender.
3. Adjust to high heat and press the corned beef mixture down in the skillet.
4. Cook within one to two mins or till the corned beef gets crispy. Switch off the heat, top using garlic powder and pepper, and serve.

Nutritional Values:

- Calories: 250
- Net Carbs: 1g
- Fat: 20g
- Protein: 16g
- Sugar: 0g

Difficulty: 1 **2** 3 4 5

Mushroom Chili Stroganoff

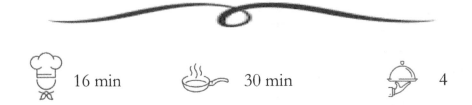

🍳 16 min   30 min   4

Ingredients:

- one tbs olive oil
- one big onion, cut
- 2 cloves garlic, crushed
- 12 oz white or cremini mushrooms, sliced
- 1 cup chili (made with ground turkey or beef and low-carb vegetables)
- 1 cup beef broth
- half cup full-fat sour cream
- Salt & pepper, as required
- two cups cooked cauliflower rice for serving

Directions:

1. Inside your big griddle, warm olive oil across moderate flame. Include the chopped onion and garlic. Cook for five mins or till the onion turns translucent.
2. Mix in mushrooms and cook within 10 mins till they begin to brown. Include the chili and cook for another min, mixing often.
3. Pour broth and let it simmer. Continue to cook for ten more mins or till slightly dense.
4. Eliminate the skillet and mix in sour cream—top utilizing salt & pepper. Serve across cauliflower rice.

Nutritional Values:

- Calories: 335
- Net Carbs: 9g
- Fat: 23g
- Protein: 20g
- Sugar: 5g

Difficulty: 1 2 3 4 5

Cabbage Skillet with Kielbasa

11 min   18 min   4

Ingredients:

- two tbsps. salted butter
- 6 cups thinly sliced cabbage
- ¼ cup sliced yellow onion
- two garlic cloves, crushed
- one pound kielbasa, shared lengthwise and sliced into quarter-inch half-moons
- two tbsp German- or Dijon-style mustard
- two tbsp apple cider vinegar
- half tsp. salt (kosher if preferred)
- quarter tsp. ground black pepper

Directions:

1. Warm the butter in your big skillet across moderate flame till just melted. Include the cabbage and cook within five mins, then include the onion and garlic.
2. Adjust to moderate-low heat and cook within ten mins till the cabbage softens.
3. Include the kielbasa and mix well. Cook within three-four mins or till the kielbasa is hot.
4. Combine the mustard and vinegar in your small container, afterwards include it to the cabbage solution, mixing thoroughly to blend. Season with salt & pepper and serve.

Nutritional Values:

- Calories: 351
- Net Carbs: 11g
- Fat: 26g
- Protein: 17g
- Sugar: 0g

Difficulty: 1 **2** 3 4 5

Orange Tofu with Broccoli

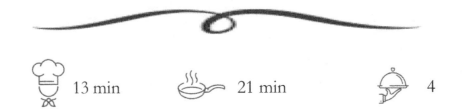

🍳 13 min   🍳 21 min   🍽 4

Ingredients:

- 14 oz firm tofu, diced
- four cups broccoli florets
- half cup sugar-free orange marmalade
- quarter cup low-sodium soy sauce
- one tbs rice vinegar
- one tsp ginger, crushed
- 3 cloves garlic, crushed
- one tablespoon olive oil
- Salt & ground pepper, as required

Directions:

1. Whisk orange marmalade, soy sauce, rice vinegar, ginger, and garlic in your small container. Put away.
2. Warm olive oil in your big griddle across moderate-high flame. Include the tofu and cook within 8 mins till browned on every end. Eliminate & put away.
3. Include the broccoli florets to your skillet and cook within 4 mins till they turn tender-crisp.
4. Stir in sauce mixture and cook for three mins or till thickened mildly. Return the cooked tofu and mix well till it is coated with sauce—top utilizing salt & pepper. Serve warm.

Nutritional Values:

- Calories: 351
- Net Carbs: 11g
- Fat: 26g
- Protein: 17g
- Sugar: 0g

Difficulty: 1 2 **3** 4 5

Cheese Stuffed Bell Peppers

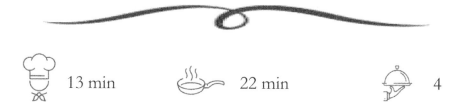

🍳 13 min   🍳 22 min   🍽 4

Ingredients:

- one tbsp. avocado oil
- ¼ cup sliced yellow onion
- two cups ricotta cheese
- ½ cup parmesan cheese
- one big egg
- one tablespoon Italian seasoning
- half tsp. kosher salt
- quarter tsp. ground black pepper
- four big bell peppers, cut in half vertically and seeded
- 1 cup store-bought sugar-free marinara sauce
- 2 cups ragged mozzarella cheese

Directions:

1. The oven should be preheated to 375°F.
2. Warm the oil inside an average griddle across moderate flame and include the onion. Cook within five mins till it is soft and translucent.
3. Combine the onion, ricotta, Parmesan, egg, Italian seasoning, salt, and pepper inside a moderate container.
4. Place two tbsps. of marinara sauce among the peppers. Nestle spoonful of ricotta mixture into each pepper. Top with mozzarella cheese.
5. Place the filled peppers inside a big casserole dish. Bake within 15 mins or till hot and bubbly. Serve.

Nutritional Values:

- Calories: 410
- Net Carbs: 8g
- Fat: 29g
- Protein: 28g
- Sugar: 6g

Difficulty: 1 2 **3** 4 5

Eggplant Parm in Sheet-Pan

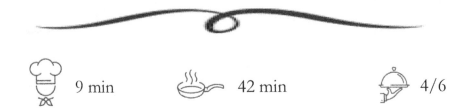

🍳 9 min   🍳 42 min   🍽 4/6

Ingredients:

- 4 tbsps. extra-virgin olive oil
- one big eggplant, cut into half-inch-thick rounds
- one teaspoon salt
- quarter tsp ground black pepper
- one and a half cups shredded Parmesan cheese
- one cup melted and drained frozen spinach
- one and a half cups no-sugar-included marinara sauce
- one cup ragged mozzarella cheese

Directions:

1. The oven should be preheated to 400 degrees F.
2. Coat the lower part of a deep sheet pot utilizing two tbsps. olive oil.
3. Position the eggplant rounds in one layer, add the remaining olive oil as a drizzle, and season with salt and pepper on top.. Roast within ten to fifteen mins till just tender.
4. Drizzle the eggplant with 1 cup of Parmesan and roast another 5 to 10 mins, or till the cheese is dissolved and golden.
5. Top the eggplant with the spinach, marinara sauce, and mozzarella, spreading evenly in layers. Top with the remaining Parmesan cheese.
6. Roast another ten-fifteen mins or till bubbly. Serve hot.

Nutritional Values:

- Calories: 442
- Net Carbs: 11g
- Fat: 33g
- Protein: 22g
- Sugar: 0g

Difficulty: 1 2 3 **4** 5

Garlic Tempeh Lettuce Wraps

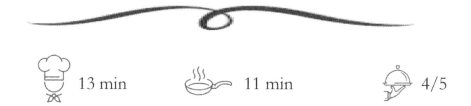

🧑‍🍳 13 min   🍳 11 min   🍽 4/5

Ingredients:

- eight oz tempeh, crumbled
- two cloves garlic, minced
- one tbsp olive oil
- quarter cup low-sodium soy sauce or tamari
- quarter cup rice vinegar

- one tsp sesame oil
- Tweak of black pepper
- two green onions, sliced
- one-third cup chopped red bell pepper
- one-third cup grated carrot
- 8 big lettuce leaves, washed and dried

Directions:

1. Heat a big griddle with olive oil across moderate flame. Include the garlic and cook within one min till fragrant.
2. Include the crumbled tempeh and cook within 5 mins, often stirring, till it starts to brown.
3. Toss the soy sauce, rice vinegar, sesame oil, and black pepper in your small container. Pour the sauce mixture across the tempeh and start to cook within three mins.
4. Remove the skillet and stir in green onions, diced red bell pepper, and grated carrot. Spoon the tempeh solution onto every lettuce leaf and wrap them like a burrito.

Nutritional Values:

- Calories: 210
- Net Carbs: 8g
- Fat: 13g
- Protein: 14g
- Sugar: 3g

Difficulty: 1 2 **3** 4 5

Zucchini Au Gratin

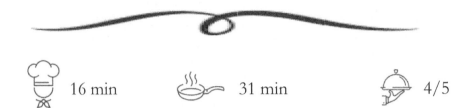

♕ 16 min   ♨ 31 min   🍽 4/5

Ingredients:

- Cooking spray or olive oil
- two big zucchini, cut into quarter-inch-dense rounds
- one teaspoon salt
- 4 oz full-fat cream cheese
- ¼ cup hefty (whipping) cream
- one tsp garlic powder
- half cup each of shredded mozzarella, Parmesan & cheddar cheese, shredded
- ¼ teaspoon ground black pepper

Directions:

1. Warm up the oven to 400°F. Grease an eight by eight-inch glass baking tray with cooking spray or coat it utilizing olive oil.
2. Organize the zucchini rounds in one layer on several paper towels and drizzle using salt.
3. Let sit for ten mins to pull the extra moisture out of the zucchini. Season with includeitional layer of paper towels to absorb the liquid.
4. Combine the cream cheese, heavy cream, and garlic powder inside a small griddle across moderate-high flame.
5. Whisking constantly, let it simmer within three-four mins till the cream cheese is dissolved and the solution is uniform.
6. Adjust to low heat and whisk in ¼ cup each of the mozzarella, Parmesan, and cheddar, blending till uniform and the cheeses are dissolved. Eliminate the skillet and cover.
7. Pour half the warm sauce into your baking dish and arrange the drained zucchini slices in rows.
8. Top with the remaining cream sauce and drizzle with the rest of the quarter cup each of mozzarella, Parmesan, and cheddar. Drizzle with the ground pepper. Serve.

Nutritional Values:

- Calories: 311
- Net Carbs: 7g
- Fat: 25g
- Protein: 14g
- Sugar: 0g

Difficulty: 1 2 3 4 **5**

Tempeh and Veggie Curry

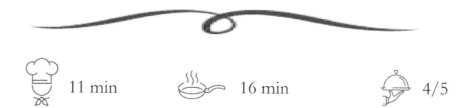

🧑‍🍳 11 min   🍳 16 min   🍽 4/5

Ingredients:

- one small yellow onion, thinly sliced
- one moderate eggplant, unpeeled & into ½-inch cubes
- 4 minced garlic cloves
- 2 tbsp coconut oil
- two tbsps extra-virgin olive oil
- two tbsp curry powder
- one teaspoon salt
- one (13.5- oz) tin of complete-fat unsweetened coconut milk
- 4 cups baby spinach leaves
- 16 oz tempeh, cut into ½-inch-thick strips or crumbled

Directions:

1. Warm coconut and olive oil inside a big stockpot across moderate-high flame. Include the onion and eggplant, then fry for five to six mins, or till the vegetables are browned and just tender.
2. Include the curry powder, salt, and garlic, and sauté another one to two mins.
3. Pour coconut milk and let it simmer. Adjust to low heat, include the spinach and tempeh, enclose, then cook for 5 mins or till the spinach is floppy. Serve warm.

Nutritional Values:

- Calories: 565
- Net Carbs: 15g
- Fat: 43g
- Protein: 27g
- Sugar: 0g

Difficulty: 1 2 **3** 4 5

Cauliflower Rice Tabbouleh

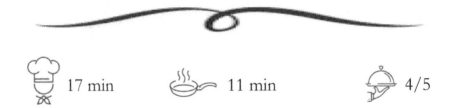

🍳 17 min   🍳 11 min   🍽 4/5

Ingredients:

- 3 cups cauliflower rice
- two cups water
- one cup diced English cucumber
- one cup shared grape tomatoes
- quarter cup sliced fresh parsley
- ¼ cup sliced scallions
- 2 tbsp lemon juice
- ¼ cup extra-virgin olive oil
- quarter tsp. salt (kosher if preferred)
- one-eighth tsp. ground black pepper

Directions:

1. Mix the cauliflower rice and water inside an average pot and boil across moderate-high flame.
2. Simmer within one min, turn off the heat, and drain the cauliflower rice. Place it in your fridge to chill for 1 hour or overnight.
3. Mix the chilled cauliflower rice, cucumber, tomatoes, parsley, and scallions inside a big container.
4. Measure the lemon juice into a small container. Toss the olive oil in a fine stream into the lemon juice to create an emulsified vinaigrette. Season the dressing utilizing salt & pepper.
5. Prior to serving, toss the cauliflower rice mixture with the vinaigrette; serve chilled.

Nutritional Values:

- Calories: 155
- Net Carbs: 4g
- Fat: 14g
- Protein: 2g
- Sugar: 0g

Difficulty: 1 2 3 **4** 5

Portobello Kung Pao

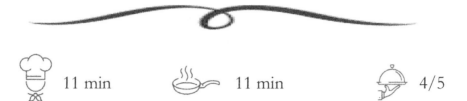

🍳 11 min   🍳 11 min   🍽 4/5

Ingredients:

- one tablespoon avocado oil
- 6 portobello mushrooms, stems removed, black gills scraped out utilizing a spatula, sliced into half-inch portions
- two scallions, both white and green portions, sliced into half-inch parts
- one green bell pepper, seeded & sliced into half-inch parts
- one cup low-sodium chicken broth
- 5 tbsps. coconut aminos (or soy sauce)
- one tbsp unseasoned rice wine vinegar
- one tablespoon brown sugar substitute
- 1 ½ tsp. sesame oil
- Kosher salt & ground black pepper as required

Directions:

1. Warm up the oil inside your big skillet across moderate-high flame. Include the diced mushrooms and cook for two to three mins, stirring frequently. Include the scallions and bell pepper, then cook for a min.
2. Meanwhile, make the sauce by mixing the chicken broth, coconut aminos, rice wine vinegar, brown sugar substitute, and sesame oil inside a moderate container.
3. When the peppers have softened, include the sauce to the griddle and turn the flame enough so that it starts to boil.
4. Simmer the sauce and vegetables for two mins or till the sauce denses a bit—top utilizing salt & pepper. Serve.

Nutritional Values:

- Calories: 97
- Net Carbs: 8g
- Fat: 5g
- Protein: 6g
- Sugar: 3g

Difficulty: 1 2 3 4 **5**

Chapter 9: Fish and Seafood

Chimichurri Tuna Steaks

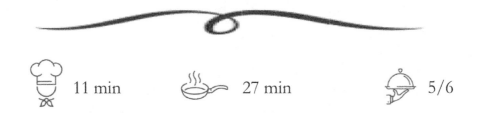

11 min   27 min   5/6

Ingredients:

- one (6-ounce) tuna steak
- ¼ cup parsley
- 1 garlic clove, sliced
- one tablespoon olive oil
- one tbsp. lemon juice
- ⅛ tsp. red pepper flakes
- Salt & black pepper, as required

Directions:

1. Include parsley, garlic, olive oil, and lemon juice in a mini mixing container, then beat till uniform.
2. Transfer the parsley solution to a container. Include the red pepper flakes, salt, plus black pepper and mix to blend. Refrigerate for almost 2 hours before cooking.
3. Warm up your oven to 350°F. Position the tuna steak in a small glass baking dish. Place the parsley solution across the tuna steak evenly. Bake for twenty-five to thirty mins till the fish simply flakes. Serve hot.

Nutritional Values:

- Calories: 313
- Net Carbs: 3g
- Fat: 14g
- Protein: 40g
- Sugar: 1g

Difficulty: 1 2 **3** 4 5

Fish Cakes with Garlic Sauce

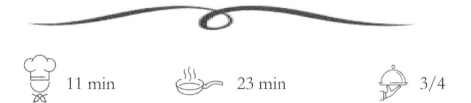

🧑‍🍳 11 min   🍳 23 min   🛎 3/4

Ingredients:

- one and a half lbs. white fish, like haddock, cod, or pollack
- 2 cups cauliflower rice
- 2 big eggs
- 1 cup superfine almond flour
- ¼ cup oat fiber
- two tbsps. sliced fresh parsley
- one scallion, sliced
- ½ tsp. kosher salt
- quarter tsp. ground black pepper
- Oil for frying
- ½ cup mayonnaise
- ½ tsp. garlic powder

Directions:

1. Warm up your oven to 375°F. Bake the fish within 12 to 15 mins on a parchment paper–lined baking sheet till it is flaky and opaque. Let the fish cool slightly.
2. In your big griddle across moderate flame, cook the cauliflower rice in ½ cup of water till the water has evaporated and the cauliflower is tender. Drain, and transfer the cauliflower to a big container.
3. Include the fish to the cauliflower, breaking it up into flakes. Include the eggs, almond flour, oat fiber, parsley, scallion, salt, and pepper, and combine thoroughly with a big spatula.
4. Form the fish mixture into about 8 patties. Heat about ½ inch of oil in a big griddle across moderate-high flame. Fry the fish cakes within 4 mins till they're golden brown. Flip them across and fry for 4 mins.
5. Inside a small container, combine the mayonnaise with the garlic powder. Serve the sauce with the hot fish cakes.

Nutritional Values:

- Calories: 548
- Net Carbs: 8g
- Fat: 40g
- Protein: 38g
- Sugar: 0g

Difficulty: 1 2 3 **4** 5

Salmon with Asparagus in Sheet Pan

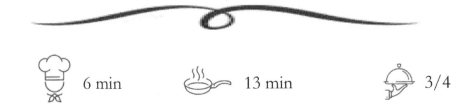

🍳 6 min   🍳 13 min   🍽 3/4

Ingredients:

- one tbsp salted butter
- four (six ounces) salmon fillets
- two tbsps. Dijon mustard
- two garlic cloves, crushed
- one tablespoon sliced fresh dill

- one tsp. kosher salt, shared
- one pound asparagus, washed & trimmed
- 2 tsp lemon pepper

Directions:

1. Warm up the oven to 350°F. Put an average sheet pan in the oven for 1 or 2 mins to warm it up.
2. Melt the butter on the warmed baking sheet. Include the salmon, leaving about 3 inches among each fillet.
3. Mix the Dijon mustard with the garlic and dill inside a small container. Brush or spread this solution uniformly across the surface of each fillet. Drizzle the fish with about ½ teaspoon salt.
4. Lay the trimmed asparagus spears on the baking sheet among and around the salmon, but keep them close together.
5. Drizzle the lemon pepper across the asparagus, then drizzle with the remaining salt. Bake for 8 mins; eliminate the baking sheet from the oven, and whip the asparagus across.
6. Bake for three to four mins till the asparagus is tender-crispy and the salmon is flaky and cooked completely.

Nutritional Values:

- Calories: 297
- Net Carbs: 2g
- Fat: 14g
- Protein: 37g
- Sugar: 0g

Difficulty: 1 2 **3** 4 5

Pan-Fried Cod with Slaw

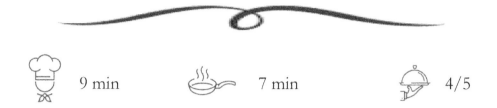

🧑‍🍳 9 min   🍳 7 min   🍽 4/5

Ingredients:

- Oil for shallow frying
- 4 (6-oz) cod fillets
- 1 cup superfine almond flour
- 1 tbsp Old Bay Seasoning
- 2 big eggs
- ½ cup mayonnaise

- two tbsps. powdered sugar substitute
- one tbsp. apple cider vinegar
- Kosher salt & ground black pepper, as required
- one (14-oz) bag of coleslaw mix

Directions:

1. Heat ¼-inch of oil inside a big griddle across moderate flame. Meanwhile, pat the fish dry with paper towels.
2. Mix the almond flour with the Old Bay seasoning inside a shallow container. Whip the eggs in a second shallow container till they're thoroughly mixed.
3. Soak the fillets into the egg and afterwards into the almond flour mixture. Press the fillets into the almond flour lightly to help the coating stick.
4. Cook the breaded fish for three-four mins or till golden brown. Carefully roll the fish across and cook for three mins or till golden brown. Put them away onto a plate.
5. Mix the mayonnaise, sugar substitute, and vinegar inside a small container. Top the dressing with salt plus pepper, toss with the coleslaw mix, and serve alongside the crispy fish fillets.

Nutritional Values:

- Calories: 471
- Net Carbs: 7g
- Fat: 33g
- Protein: 33g
- Sugar: 6g

Difficulty: 1 2 3 **4** 5

Mediterranean Poached Tuna

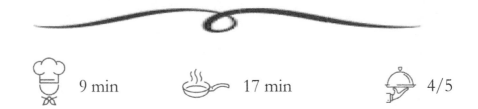

🍳 9 min   🍳 17 min   🍽 4/5

Ingredients:

- ½ small yellow onion, minced
- 8 garlic cloves, peeled & smashed
- 10 Kalamata olives, halved
- 10 cherry tomatoes, halved
- ½ cup + two tbsps. extra-virgin olive oil, shared
- one (14-oz) tin of quartered artichoke hearts, drained
- 1 tbsp Italian seasoning
- one tsp. salt
- half tsp. ground black pepper
- one cup chicken or vegetable stock, + more if needed
- 4 (3- to 4-oz) tuna medallions

Directions:

1. Warm two tbsp of olive oil in your moderate pot across moderate-high flame. Include the onion and sauté for 4 to 5 mins or till tender.
2. Include the garlic, artichoke hearts, olives, tomatoes, Italian seasoning, salt, and pepper, and sauté for two to three mins, till the mixture is fragrant and the tomatoes are tender.
3. Include the stock and rest of the ½ cup of olive oil and let it boil.
4. Adjust to low heat and include the tuna medallions in one layer, pushing down to submerge them in the liquid, including additional stock if necessary.
5. Cover and cook within ten-fifteen mins across low heat till the fish flakes easily. Serve.

Nutritional Values:

- Calories: 475
- Net Carbs: 7g
- Fat: 38g
- Protein: 26g
- Sugar: 0g

Difficulty: 1   2   **3**   4   5

Garlic Butter Shrimp with Veg

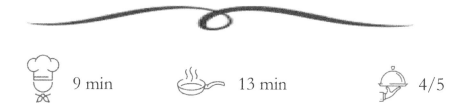

9 min   13 min   4/5

Ingredients:

- two tbsps. salted butter, divided
- one-pound (31/35 count) big shrimp, peeled & deveined
- 2 moderate zucchini, halved lengthwise & slice into **one-third**-inch-dense half-moons
- one red bell pepper, sowed and chopped finely
- one garlic clove, crushed
- ½ cup low-sodium chicken broth
- one tbsp sliced fresh dill
- ¼ teaspoon kosher salt
- ground black pepper, as required

Directions:

1. Inside a big griddle, warm 1 tbsp butter across moderate flame till melted. Include the shrimp and cook within two to three mins each end till they're pink. Set them aside, leaving any liquid behind in the skillet.
2. Include the zucchini, bell pepper, and garlic to the griddle—fry for 3 to 4 mins or till the zucchini softens.
3. Include the chicken broth, dill, salt, and pepper. Boil for 2 to 3 more mins or till the veggies are softer.
4. Return the shrimp to your skillet and cook till heated thoroughly. Serve immediately.

Nutritional Values:

- Calories: 168
- Net Carbs: 5g
- Fat: 8g
- Protein: 18g
- Sugar: 0g

Difficulty: 1 2 **3** 4 5

Clam Cauliflower Chowder

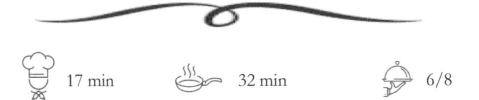

🧑‍🍳 17 min   🍳 32 min   🍽 6/8

Ingredients:

- four cups sliced cauliflower
- one cup sliced celery
- one average onion, thinly sliced
- two (ten ounces each) cans of baby clams, drained & juice reserved
- four cups low-sodium chicken broth
- one cup unsweetened almond milk
- one cup heavy cream
- four tbsps. unsalted butter
- two garlic cloves, crushed
- one tsp dried thyme
- Salt & pepper, as required
- Chopped fresh parsley for garnish

Directions:

1. Inside your big pot across moderate flame, melt the butter. Include the onions and celery and cook within five mins till softened. Include the garlic and cook within another min till fragrant.
2. Pour chicken broth, clam juice, milk, and heavy cream. Stir well.
3. Include the cauliflower and dried thyme, then top utilizing salt & pepper. Let it boil, adjust to low heat, and simmer within twenty mins or till the cauliflower is softer.
4. Purée the soup utilizing your immersion mixer till uniform. Stir in canned baby clams, then cook for five mins till warmed up completely. Regulate salt and pepper as required. Garnish with parsley, and serve warm.

Nutritional Values:

- Calories: 290
- Net Carbs: 6g
- Fat: 22g
- Protein: 14g
- Sugar: 4g

Difficulty: 1 2 3 **4** 5

Seared Scallops with Spring Veg

🍳 17 min   🍳 12 min   🍽 4/6

Ingredients:

- 12 big scallops, patted dry
- Salt & pepper, as required
- two tbsp olive oil
- 1 cup asparagus, chopped into one-inch parts
- one cup cherry tomatoes, halved
- one cup zucchini, cut into half-moons
- two cloves garlic, crushed
- quarter cup white wine vinegar (optional)
- 2 tbsps. butter or ghee
- Fresh parsley, sliced for garnish

Directions:

1. Top the scallops utilizing salt plus pepper on each ends—warm olive oil in your big skillet across moderate-high flame.
2. Sear the scallops for two mins on every end till cooked thoroughly. Transfer to a plate and keep warm.
3. Include asparagus, cherry tomatoes, zucchini, and garlic in the same skillet. Cook within 5 mins or till vegetables are softer.
4. Deglaze the pan with white wine vinegar (if utilizing). Stir in butter and cook till blended.
5. Return the scallops to your skillet and allow them to warm through for about a min. Garnish with parsley, and serve.

Nutritional Values:

- Calories: 210
- Net Carbs: 5g
- Fat: 14g
- Protein: 15g
- Sugar: 2g

Difficulty: 1 **2** 3 4 5

Coconut-Curry Shrimp

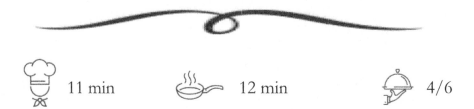

🍳 11 min   🍳 12 min   🍽 4/6

Ingredients:

- two tbsps. avocado oil
- ½ cup sliced red onion
- one (one-inch) piece ginger, crushed
- 1 garlic clove, crushed
- one and a half pounds (21/25 count) big shrimp, skinned & deveined
- one red bell pepper, sowed and cut
- one (14-oz) can of full-fat coconut milk
- one tsp Thai red curry paste
- one tbsp. lime juice
- Kosher salt & ground black pepper, as required
- Cilantro, sliced peanuts, chopped Thai basil, or sliced scallions to garnish

Directions:

1. Warm the oil in your big skillet across moderate flame. Include the onion, ginger, and garlic and sauté for two-three mins or till the onions start to softer.
2. Include the shrimp and bell pepper, cook for two to three mins, then role the shrimp across. Start cooking within two mins or till the shrimp are pink and opaque.
3. Include the coconut milk plus red curry paste. Mix well to combine. Include the lime juice, then top utilizing salt & pepper. Garnish with your favorite toppings and serve.

Nutritional Values:

- Calories: 394
- Net Carbs: 7g
- Fat: 30g
- Protein: 26g
- Sugar: 0g

Difficulty: 1 **2** 3 4 5

Chapter 10: Chicken And Turkey

Chicken Broccoli Alfredo

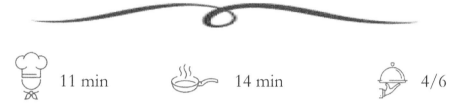

11 min   14 min   4/6

Ingredients:

- 1 tablespoon avocado oil
- one-lb. boneless, skinless chicken breast, cut into half-inch-thick slices
- ½ tsp kosher salt
- ¼ tsp ground black pepper
- 1 tbsp salted butter
- one garlic clove, crushed
- one (sixteen-ounces) bag of sliced frozen broccoli
- 2 cups heavy cream
- quarter cup grated parmesan cheese, + more for serving

Directions:

1. Warm the oil in your big skillet across moderate flame. Top the chicken with salt plus pepper.
2. Include the chicken, then cook for 6 to 8 mins or till it is fully cooked and no longer pink inside.
3. Include the butter and garlic, then cook for 1 min or till the garlic is fragrant. Include the broccoli and cook within 2 mins to thaw the broccoli.
4. Include the cream and raise the mixture to a simmer. Simmer for 3 mins to thicken slightly, then turn off the heat.
5. Include the parmesan cheese and mix thoroughly. Serve with extra parmesan and a few grinds of ground black pepper.

Nutritional Values:

- Calories: 663
- Net Carbs: 8g
- Fat: 55g
- Protein: 33g
- Sugar: 0g

Difficulty: 1 2 3 **4** 5

One-Pan Lemon Herbed Chicken

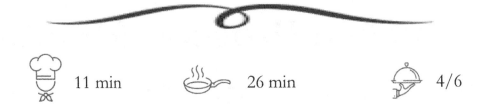

🧑‍🍳 11 min   🍳 26 min   🍽 4/6

Ingredients:

- 4 tbsp extra-virgin olive oil, shared
- one-lb. boneless skinless chicken thighs
- 1 teaspoon salt
- half teaspoon ground black pepper
- 2 tbsps. Italian or Greek seasoning
- 8 garlic cloves, peeled and smashed
- 1 lemon, thinly sliced

Directions:

1. Preheat the oven to 425°F.
2. Cover your eight-by-eight-inch glass baking dish with 2 tbsp olive oil. Put the chicken and drizzle with the salt, pepper, and Italian seasoning.
3. Season the chicken with the smashed garlic cloves and lemon slices. Sprinkle with the remaining olive oil.
4. Roast within twenty-five to thirty mins or till the chicken has cooked thoroughly. Remove, discard the lemon slices, and serve warm.

Nutritional Values:

- Calories: 266
- Net Carbs: 2g
- Fat: 21g
- Protein: 19g
- Sugar: 0g

Difficulty: 1 **2** 3 4 5

Coconut Curry Chicken

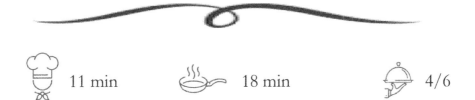

🍳 11 min   🍳 18 min   🍽 4/6

Ingredients:

- one tbsp avocado oil
- ½ cup sliced red onion
- one garlic clove, minced
- one tbsp peeled & grated fresh ginger
- 1½ tbsp yellow curry powder
- one (fifteen-ounces) can of full-fat coconut milk
- quarter cup water
- 2 tbsp sugar-free ketchup or tomato paste
- one-lb. boneless, skinless chicken breast sliced into strips
- Kosher salt & ground black pepper as required

Directions:

1. Warm the oil in your big skillet across moderate flame. Include the onion, then cook within 4 mins till it softens.
2. Include the garlic plus ginger, then cook for one min or till aromatic, then mix in the curry powder.
3. Meanwhile, whisk the coconut milk, water, and ketchup inside a moderate container. Include the mixture to the skillet, adjust to low heat, and simmer for five mins, till the liquid has reduced a bit.
4. Include the chicken and cook within six-eight mins across moderate flame till the chicken is cooked—season with salt and pepper. Serve.

Nutritional Values:

- Calories: 386
- Net Carbs: 6g
- Fat: 28g
- Protein: 28g
- Sugar: 0g

Difficulty: 1 2 **3** 4 5

Garlic Butter Chicken with Cauliflower Rice

🍳 11 min   ♨ 16 min   🍽 4/6

Ingredients:

- 4 tbsp cold salted butter, shared
- one-lb. boneless, skinless chicken breast, sliced into one-inch cubes
- 1 tsp kosher salt, divided
- ¼ tsp ground black pepper
- 2 garlic cloves, crushed
- ½ cup low-sodium chicken broth
- three cups cauliflower rice
- ¼ cup water
- two tbsps. chopped fresh parsley
- ¼ tsp paprika

Directions:

1. Inside your big skillet across moderate flame, dissolve two tbsps. of butter.
2. Season the chicken with ½ tsp salt and pepper. Include the chicken to your skillet and cook across moderate flame within three-four mins.
3. Flip the chicken and cook within three-four mins or till cooked completely. Put it away on a plate.
4. Include the garlic to your skillet and cook for one min or till aromatic. Include the chicken broth and simmer within 4 mins till diminished by half.
5. Meanwhile, put the cauliflower rice, water, and remaining salt in oven-safe container, cacross it with plastic wrap, and cook on high for three mins or till the cauliflower is tender. Stir it and drain.
6. Turn the heat off and include the rest of the cold butter, swirling to melt the butter slowly.
7. Return the chicken to your skillet with any juices from the plate, and top with the parsley and paprika. Serve the chicken with a spoonful of sauce on a bed of cauliflower rice.

Nutritional Values:

- Calories: 254
- Net Carbs: 3g
- Fat: 14g
- Protein: 28g
- Sugar: 0g

Difficulty: 1 2 **3** 4 5

One-Pot Chicken Margherita

🧑‍🍳 11 min   🍳 18 min   🍽️ 4/6

Ingredients:

- four (4- ounces) boneless, skinless chicken thighs
- ½ teaspoon salt
- quarter teaspoon ground black pepper
- 4 tbsp extra-virgin olive oil, divided
- ½ cup no-sugar-added marinara sauce, such as Rao's
- 2 ounces fresh mozzarella, sliced into four ½-inch thick slices
- 4 to 8 big, fresh basil leaves

Directions:

1. Drizzle the chicken with salt and pepper.
2. Warm 2 tbsp olive oil in your big skillet with a lid across moderate-high flame. Include the chicken, then brown on every end within three to four mins each end.
3. Spoon 2 tbsp marinara sauce atop each thigh and top each with 1 mozzarella slice. Cover, adjust to low heat, and simmer within eight to ten mins till the chicken is cooked.
4. Top the chicken with the basil leaves to taste and sprinkle with the rest of the olive oil. Serve warm.

Nutritional Values:

- Calories: 314
- Net Carbs: 2g
- Fat: 22g
- Protein: 25g
- Sugar: 0g

Difficulty: 1 **2** 3 4 5

Ground Turkey Lettuce Wrap

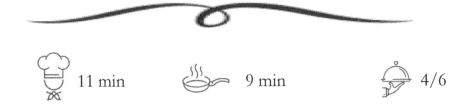

🍳 11 min   🍲 9 min   🍽 4/6

Ingredients:

- one tablespoon avocado oil
- 2 tbsps. peeled & grated fresh ginger
- one garlic clove, crushed
- one-pound lean ground turkey
- ¼ cup low-sodium chicken broth
- one tablespoon sugar-free fish sauce (optional)

- two tbsps. lime juice
- one teaspoon brown sugar substitute
- 1 tablespoon natural peanut butter
- 8 big lettuce leaves, romaine, butter lettuce, or iceberg

Directions:

1. Heat the oil in your big skillet across moderate flame. Include the ginger plus garlic, then cook for 1 to 2 mins, till fragrant.
2. Include the ground turkey, and mix it with the ginger and garlic. Cook within five-six mins or till the turkey is no longer pink.
3. Meanwhile, inside a small container, mix the chicken broth, fish sauce, lime juice, and peanut butter. Include this mixture to the ground turkey, and cook within 2 to 3 mins or till most liquid evaporates.
4. Include **one-third** cup of the turkey mixture to a lettuce cup, and top it with your favorite diabetic-friendly garnishes. Serve.

Nutritional Values:

- Calories: 237
- Net Carbs: 2g
- Fat: 15g
- Protein: 23g
- Sugar: 1g

Difficulty: 1 **2** 3 4 5

Lean Turkey Meatballs

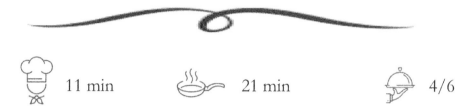

🎩 11 min   🍳 21 min   🍽 4/6

Ingredients:

- one-pound lean ground turkey
- ¼ cup almond flour
- ¼ cup chopped onion
- one big egg
- one teaspoon minced garlic

- half teaspoon chopped fresh thyme
- ¼ teaspoon sea salt
- one-eighth teaspoon ground nutmeg
- ⅛ tsp ground black pepper

Directions:

1. Warm up the oven to 400 degrees F. Line a baking sheet with parchment paper.
2. Combine the turkey, almond flour, onion, egg, garlic, thyme, salt, nutmeg, and pepper in your big container. Form the mixture into one-inch meatballs.
3. Bake within 20 mins, turning halfway through, till cooked through and browned.

Nutritional Values:

- Calories: 228
- Net Carbs: 3g
- Fat: 13g
- Protein: 24g
- Sugar: 1g

Difficulty: 1 **2** 3 4 5

Sweet and Sour Turkey

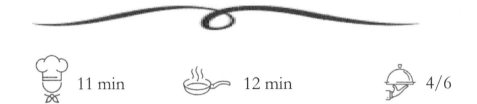

🧑‍🍳 11 min   🍳 12 min   🍽 4/6

Ingredients:

- 1-pound boneless, skinless turkey breast, cut into one-inch cubes
- ½ teaspoon kosher salt
- ¼ tsp ground black pepper
- 1 tbsp avocado oil
- one green bell pepper, seeded & sliced into strips
- ½ cup sliced red onion
- quarter cup water
- 2 tbsp sugar-free ketchup
- 2 tbsp brown sugar substitute
- 2 tbsp apple cider vinegar

Directions:

1. Top the turkey with salt and pepper.
2. Warm the oil in your big skillet across moderate flame. Include the turkey cubes, and cook within for five to six mins across moderate flame, stirring often, or till it is no longer pink inside.
3. Include the green bell pepper and onion, then cook within two to three mins or till the vegetables start to soften.
4. In the meantime, in your small container, whisk simultaneously the water, sugar-free ketchup, brown sugar substitute, and apple cider vinegar.
5. Once the turkey is cooked, include the sauce to your skillet and heat it within 3 mins, stirring often. Serve with cauliflower rice or your favorite low-carb vegetables.

Nutritional Values:

- Calories: 173
- Net Carbs: 2g
- Fat: 5g
- Protein: 27g
- Sugar: 6g

Difficulty: 1 2 3 **4** 5

Turkey Enchilada Bowl

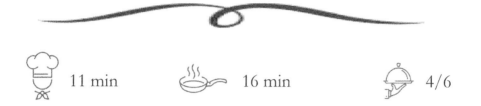

🧑‍🍳 11 min   🍳 16 min   🍽 4/6

Ingredients:

- one tbsp avocado oil
- one-lb. lean ground turkey
- quarter cup chopped yellow onion
- 8 ounces of tinned tomato puree
- half cup low-sodium chicken broth
- one tbsp chili powder
- one teaspoon ground cumin

- half teaspoon chipotle powder
- half teaspoon garlic powder
- Kosher salt & ground black pepper, as required
- Cheese, chopped cilantro, diced avocado, sliced jalapeños, or sour cream (for garnish)

Directions:

1. In your big skillet across moderate flame, heat the oil. Include the ground turkey and cook for 3 to 4 mins, till it starts to brown.
2. Include the onion and cook within five-six mins, till the ground turkey is no longer pink.
3. Include the canned tomato puree, chicken broth, chili powder, cumin, chipotle powder, and garlic powder.
4. Mix well and let it simmer across low heat for three-four mins, then season with salt and pepper. Serve topped with your favorite garnishes.

Nutritional Values:

- Calories: 233
- Net Carbs: 5g
- Fat: 13g
- Protein: 24g
- Sugar: 0g

Difficulty: 1 2 3 **4** 5

Zoodles with Beef Meatballs

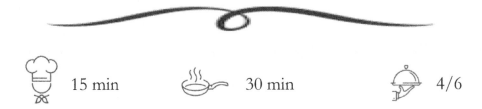

15 min   30 min   4/6

Ingredients:

- 2 tbsp extra-virgin olive oil
- 1 pound ground beef, preferably grass-fed
- 2 tsp garlic powder and onion powder
- 1 tsp salt
- ¼ tsp ground black pepper
- ½ cup grated Parmesan cheese, + extra for serving
- 1 jar of no-sugar-added marinara sauce, such as Rao's
- 8 cups spiralized zucchini (from 2 to 3 big zucchini)

Directions:

1. Preheat the oven to 375°F. Line a rimmed baking sheet utilizing aluminum foil and coat it with olive oil.
2. Combine the beef, garlic powder, onion powder, salt, pepper, and Parmesan cheese in your big container. Utilizing your hands, mix till well incorporated, then form into 1-inch-round meatballs.
3. Arrange the meatballs on your baking sheet. Bake within 18 to 20 mins or till meatballs are browned on the outside.
4. Transfer the meatballs and any rendered liquid to a moderate saucepan. Include the marinara sauce and let it boil, then adjust to low heat, cover, and simmer for 5 to 10 mins to develop the flavors.
5. Transfer 2 cups of zoodles to each of 4 containers and top with a quarter of the meatballs and the warm sauce. Garnish with additional Parmesan cheese.

Nutritional Values:

- Calories: 486
- Net Carbs: 12g
- Fat: 35g
- Protein: 29g
- Sugar: 0g

Difficulty: 1 2 3 **4** 5

California Burger Wraps

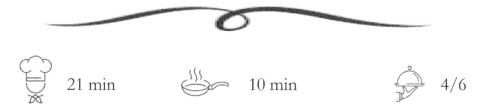

🧑‍🍳 21 min   🍳 10 min   🍽 4/6

Ingredients:

- 1-pound ground beef (80% lean, 20% fat)
- 4 big lettuce leaves (such as romaine or butter lettuce)
- 1 moderate avocado, sliced
- 1 moderate tomato, sliced
- 1/2 cup shredded cheddar cheese
- 4 slices of bacon, cooked & crumbled
- Salt & pepper, to taste

Directions:

1. In your big container, season the ground beef with salt plus pepper. Form it into four burger patties.
2. Heat your non-stick skillet across moderate-high heat. Cook the patties within 5 mins on each side till browned.
3. Lay out the lettuce leaves on a flat surface, then include one burger patty to each leaf. Top with avocado, tomato, cheddar cheese, and crumbled bacon.
4. Carefully fold the lettuce leaf around the burger to wrap. Serve.

Nutritional Values:

- Calories: 476
- Net Carbs: 5g
- Fat: 37g
- Protein: 30g
- Sugar: 2g

Difficulty: 1 **2** 3 4 5

Flank Streaks with Creamy Pepper Sauce

10 min   20 min   4/6

Ingredients:

- 1 pound flank steak
- 2 tsp salt, divided
- 1 tsp ground black pepper, divided
- 2 tbsp extra-virgin olive oil
- 3 tbsp unsalted butter, divided

- 1 big shallot (or ¼ small red onion), finely minced
- 2 garlic cloves, minced
- ¼ cup dry white wine or beef broth
- 2 tsp dried thyme
- ½ cup heavy (whipping) cream

Directions:

1. Season the steak with 1 tsp salt and ¼ tsp pepper. Let sit at room temperature within 10 mins.
2. Heat the olive oil and 1 tbsp butter in a big skillet across moderate-high heat. Include the steak and sear within 3 to 4 mins per side till browned.
3. Adjust to moderate heat, cover, and cook for 3 to 4 mins or till steak is moderate-rare. Remove and cover to keep warm.
4. Include the remaining butter to your skillet and melt across moderate heat. Include the shallot, garlic, remaining salt, and pepper, and sauté for 1 to 2 mins.
5. Whisk in white wine and thyme, then simmer within 2 to 3 mins till the liquid has evaporated by half.
6. Whisk in heavy cream, let it simmer, and cook, whisking constantly, till thick and creamy. Serve the steak warm with cream sauce.

Nutritional Values:

- Calories: 447
- Net Carbs: 3g
- Fat: 35g
- Protein: 26g
- Sugar: 0g

Difficulty: 1 2 3 **4** 5

Spinach Goat Cheese Stuffed Pork Loin

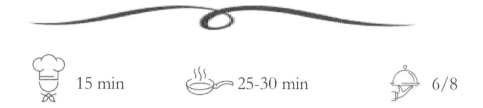

🧑‍🍳 15 min   🍳 25-30 min   🛎 6/8

Ingredients:

- 1 to 1½ pounds of pork tenderloin
- 4 oz crumbled goat cheese
- 2 cups frozen spinach, thawed and well drained
- 2 tbsp chopped sun-dried tomatoes
- ½ tsp salt
- ¼ tsp ground black pepper
- 4 tbsp extra-virgin olive oil, divided

Directions:

1. Preheat the oven to 375°F. Make a deep incision along the length of the tenderloin, leaving 1 inch on each side. Create a deep pocket without cutting all the way through to the other side.
2. Combine the goat cheese, spinach, tomatoes, salt, pepper, and 2 tbsp olive oil in your moderate container.
3. Stuff the mixture into the tenderloin pocket, pressing to seal the meat around the filling. Rub the remaining olive oil on the outside of the meat and put it in a glass baking dish.
4. Cover utilizing aluminum foil and bake within 20 to 25 mins. Uncover and bake within 5 to 10 mins or till golden brown. Serve.

Nutritional Values:

- Calories: 290
- Net Carbs: 1g
- Fat: 17g
- Protein: 30g
- Sugar: 0g

Difficulty: 1 2 **3** 4 5

Baked Bratwurst with Sauerkraut

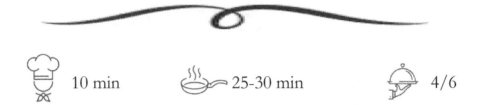

🍳 10 min   🍳 25-30 min   🍽 4/6

Ingredients:

- 16 oz sauerkraut, drained
- ¼ cup thinly sliced yellow onion
- 1 tbsp brown sugar substitute
- 1 tsp garlic powder
- ½ tsp kosher salt
- ¼ tsp ground black pepper
- 1 pound bratwurst sausage links

Directions:

1. Preheat the oven to 375°F.
2. Mix the sauerkraut with the sliced onion, brown sugar substitute, garlic powder, salt, and pepper in a moderate container.
3. Arrange the sauerkraut mixture in your 8-inch square casserole dish. Lay the bratwurst on top.
4. Cover and bake in the middle of the oven for 15 mins, then take it out and stir the sauerkraut around.
5. Put the baking dish back in your oven, and bake for 15 mins uncover or till the sausages are cooked. Serve.

Nutritional Values:

- Calories: 196
- Net Carbs: 4g
- Fat: 10g
- Protein: 19g
- Sugar: 3g

Difficulty: 1 2 **3** 4 5

Pork Chops with Creamy Mushroom Sauce

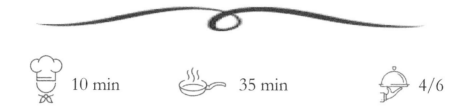

🧑‍🍳 10 min   🍳 35 min   🍽 4/6

Ingredients:

- 2 tbsp extra-virgin olive oil
- 4 (4- oz) boneless pork chops
- 2 tsp salt, divided
- ½ tsp freshly ground black pepper, divided
- 1 tbsp unsalted butter
- 4 oz chopped mushrooms
- 2 garlic cloves, minced
- 1 tsp dried thyme
- 8 oz full-fat cream cheese at room temperature
- ½ cup heavy (whipping) cream
- ¼ cup chicken stock

Directions:

1. Preheat the oven to 375°F.
2. Drizzle the olive oil in your 8-by-8-inch glass baking dish and arrange the pork chops in one layer. Drizzle with 1 tsp salt and ¼ tsp pepper.
3. Melt the butter in your moderate saucepan across moderate heat. Include the mushrooms and sauté within 3 to 4 mins till just tender.
4. Include the garlic, thyme, and cream cheese, and stir till melted. Whisk in cream, stock, and remaining salt and pepper, then cook within 3 to 4 mins or till thick and creamy.
5. Pour the mushroom sauce across the pork chops and cover them with aluminum foil. Bake within 20 to 25 mins or till the pork is cooked through.

Nutritional Values:

- Calories: 525
- Net Carbs: 5g
- Fat: 45g
- Protein: 29g
- Sugar: 0g

Difficulty: 1 2 3 4 5

Pork and Green Bean Stir-Fry

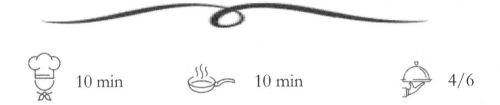

🧑‍🍳 10 min   🍳 10 min   🍽 4/6

Ingredients:

- 1-pound green beans, trimmed
- 1 tbsp avocado oil
- 1-pound lean ground pork
- ¼ cup sliced red onion
- 1 clove garlic, minced
- 1 tbsp peeled & grated fresh ginger
- 1 red bell pepper, seeded & cut into strips
- ¼ cup low-sodium chicken broth
- 3 tbsp coconut aminos
- 1 tsp sesame oil

Directions:

1. Boil your big pot of salted water across high heat and include the beans. Boil for 1 min, drain, and chill them in a big container of ice water. Drain the beans and set them aside.
2. Meanwhile, heat the oil in your big skillet across moderate heat. Include the ground pork and cook for 3 to 4 mins, breaking it up till it is no longer pink.
3. Include the onion, garlic, and ginger, then cook within 2 mins or till aromatic. Stir in the bell pepper, blanched green beans, and chicken broth.
4. Adjust to moderate-high heat and cook till the vegetables are heated through, and the broth is mostly evaporated. Include the coconut aminos and sesame oil. Mix well and serve.

Nutritional Values:

- Calories: 397
- Net Carbs: 8g
- Fat: 29g
- Protein: 23g
- Sugar: 0g

Difficulty: 1 2 **3** 4 5

Herbed Lamb Chops

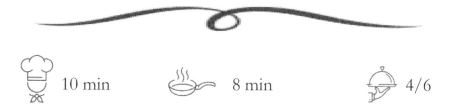

10 min   8 min   4/6

Ingredients:

- 8 lamb rib chops, trimmed
- 2 tbsp extra virgin olive oil
- 4 cloves garlic, minced
- 1 tbsp fresh rosemary leaves, chopped
- 1 tbsp fresh thyme leaves, chopped
- 1 tsp kosher salt
- 1/2 tsp ground black pepper
- Zest of one lemon

Directions:

1. Mix the olive oil, minced garlic, rosemary, thyme, salt, pepper, and lemon zest in your small container. Set aside.
2. Pat the lamb chops dry, then season both sides with the herb mixture. Allow them to marinate in the refrigerator for at least 30 mins or up to two hours.
3. Preheat your grill pan to moderate-high heat. Grill the lamb chops within 3 to 4 mins per side till they develop a nice crust.
4. Remove the lamb chops and let them rest for a few mins before serving.

Nutritional Values:

- Calories: 388
- Net Carbs: 1g
- Fat: 34g
- Protein: 21g
- Sugar: 0g

Difficulty: 1 2 **3** 4 5

Lime Lamb Cutlets

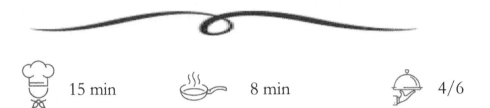

🍳 15 min   🍳 8 min   🍽 4/6

Ingredients:

- ¼ cup freshly squeezed lime juice
- 2 tbsp lime zest
- 2 tbsp chopped fresh parsley
- Sea salt & ground black pepper, to taste
- 1 tbsp extra-virgin olive oil
- 12 (about 1½ pounds) lamb cutlets

Directions:

1. Combine the lime juice, zest, parsley, salt, black pepper, and olive oil in your big container. Include the lamb cutlets, then toss to coat well.
2. Wrap the container in plastic and refrigerate to marinate for at least 4 hours. Preheat the oven to 450°F. Line a baking sheet with aluminum foil.
3. Remove the container from the refrigerator and let sit for 10 mins, then discard the marinade.
4. Arrange the lamb cutlets on the baking sheet. Broil the lamb for 8 mins, flipping once. Serve.

Nutritional Values:

- Calories: 297
- Net Carbs: 0g
- Fat: 18g
- Protein: 31g
- Sugar: 0g

Difficulty: 1 2 3 **4** 5

Lamb Peppers Lettuce Cups

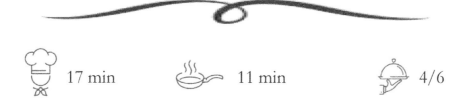

🧑‍🍳 17 min   🍳 11 min   🍽 4/6

Ingredients:

- one-pound ground lamb
- 1 tablespoon olive oil
- half cup sliced onion
- two cloves garlic, crushed
- half cup sliced red bell pepper
- quarter cup sliced fresh cilantro
- quarter cup sliced fresh mint
- quarter cup sliced fresh parsley
- one tbsp lemon juice
- Salt & pepper, to taste
- 12 big lettuce leaves
- Optional toppings: sliced avocado, crumbled feta cheese, diced cucumber

Directions:

1. In your big skillet, heat the olive oil across moderate heat. Include the onion and cook within 5 mins till softened. Include the ground lamb, breaking it up till slightly browned.
2. When the lamb is almost cooked through, include the garlic and red bell pepper. Cook within 2 to 3 mins till the lamb is fully cooked.
3. Remove and cool it down before including the cilantro, mint, parsley, and lemon juice. Mix well, then season with salt and pepper.
4. To serve, spoon the lamb mixture into each lettuce leaf and top with desired toppings.

Nutritional Values:

- Calories: 310
- Net Carbs: 4g
- Fat: 22g
- Protein: 23g
- Sugar: 2g

Difficulty: 1 2 3 **4** 5

Avocado Broccoli Soup

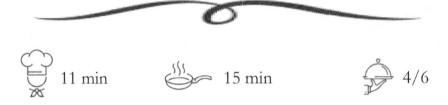

11 min   15 min   4/6

Ingredients:

- one big avocado, pitted & peeled
- 4 cups fresh broccoli florets
- 2 cups of no-salt chicken or vegetable broth
- one average onion, sliced
- 2 cloves garlic, crushed
- 1 tbsp olive oil
- one tsp ground cumin
- Salt & pepper, as required

Directions:

1. In your big pan, warm the olive oil across moderate flame. Include onion and cook within 3 mins till translucent. Include garlic and cook for another min.
2. Include broccoli and broth, and let it boil. Adjust to moderate-low flame and simmer within ten mins or till the broccoli is softer. Remove and allow it to cool for a few mins.
3. Inside a blender, mix the avocado with 1/2 broccoli mixture. Blend till smooth.
4. Pour the mixed solution back into your pot with the remaining broccoli mixture. Include ground cumin and salt, and pepper.
5. Gently reheat the soup across low heat till warm. Serve.

Nutritional Values:

- Calories: 192
- Net Carbs: 8g
- Fat: 13g
- Protein: 7g
- Sugar: 4g

Difficulty: 1 2 **3** 4 5

Creamy Tomato and Basil Soup

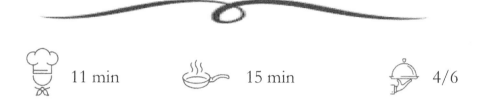

🧑‍🍳 11 min   🍳 15 min   🛎 4/6

Ingredients:

- quarter cup extra-virgin olive oil, divided
- 1 small yellow onion, sliced
- three cups chopped fresh tomatoes
- 4 garlic cloves, minced
- one teaspoon salt

- half teaspoon ground black pepper
- 1 cup chicken or vegetable stock
- ½ cup heavy (whipping) cream
- ½ cup chopped fresh basil
- 2 tbsp balsamic vinegar

Directions:

1. Warm the olive oil in your big pot across moderate-high flame. Include the onion and fry for four-six mins or till softer.
2. Include tomatoes, garlic, salt, and pepper, and fry for three-four mins till the vegetables are softer.
3. Include the stock and allow it to boil. Regulate to low flame, cover, and simmer for four-five mins or till the tomatoes have softened.
4. Remove the pan and whisk in heavy cream, basil, and balsamic vinegar. Utilizing an immersion mixer, puree till uniform and creamy. Serve warm.

Nutritional Values:

- Calories: 179
- Net Carbs: 6g
- Fat: 16g
- Protein: 2g
- Sugar: 0g

Difficulty: 1 **2** 3 4 5

Garlicky Mushroom Soup

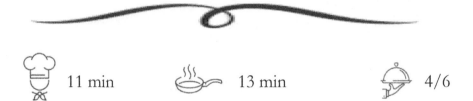

🍳 11 min   🍲 13 min   🍽 4/6

Ingredients:

- 6 tbsp extra-virgin olive oil, divided
- 1 small yellow onion, very thinly sliced
- 16 oz sliced mushrooms, divided
- 8 garlic cloves, thinly sliced
- one teaspoon salt

- quarter teaspoon ground black pepper
- 1 teaspoon dried rosemary
- two cups vegetable stock
- ¼ cup heavy (whipping) cream

Directions:

1. Warm 2 tbsp olive oil inside a moderate pot across moderate flame. Include the onion and sauté for 2 to 3 mins or till tender.
2. Include the mushrooms, garlic, salt, pepper, and rosemary, and fry for 5-6 mins or till the mushrooms are softer.
3. Include the stock, adjust to high heat, and let it boil. Adjust to low heat, cover, and simmer for 3 to 4 mins or till the vegetables are softer.
4. Remove the pan and whisk in the heavy cream till smooth. Split the soup among four containers and drizzle each with 1 tbsp olive oil. Serve hot.

Nutritional Values:

- Calories: 279
- Net Carbs: 8g
- Fat: 26g
- Protein: 5g
- Sugar: 0g

Difficulty: 1 **2** 3 4 5

Roasted Carrot Leek Soup

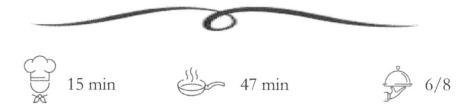

🧑‍🍳 15 min   🍳 47 min   🍽️ 6/8

Ingredients:

- one-pound carrots, peeled & chopped
- 2 leeks, cleaned & sliced
- four cloves garlic, crushed
- three tbsps. olive oil
- Salt & pepper, as required
- 4 cups low-sodium vegetable broth
- 1 cup heavy cream

Directions:

1. Warm up the oven to 400°F.
2. Whisk carrots, leeks, and garlic with olive oil in your big container. Top utilizing salt & pepper.
3. Disperse vegetables on a baking sheet in one layer. Roast within 25-30 mins till they are tender.
4. In your big pot, combine roasted vegetables and broth across moderate flame. Cook within 10 mins till warmed thoroughly. Blend the soup utilizing your immersion mixer till uniform.
5. Mix in the heavy cream, and adjust the seasoning with salt and pepper. Serve.

Nutritional Values:

- Calories: 250
- Net Carbs: 7g
- Fat: 21g
- Protein: 3g
- Sugar: 4g

Difficulty: 1 **2** 3 4 5

Egg Drop Soup

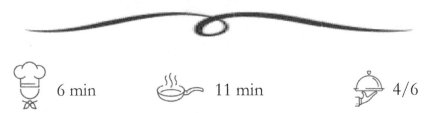

🍳 6 min   🍳 11 min   🍽 4/6

Ingredients:

- four cups low-sodium chicken broth
- 3 big eggs
- 1/4 cup chopped scallions
- two tsps. fresh minced ginger
- one tablespoon low-sodium soy sauce
- two tsps. sesame oil
- 1/2 teaspoon white pepper
- Salt, as needed

Directions:

1. Inside your moderate pan, include the broth and allow it to boil. Adjust to moderate heat and let it simmer.
2. In your small container, whisk the three big eggs till well beaten.
3. Slowly pour the whisked eggs into the pot while stirring to create egg ribbons.
4. Include the ginger, soy sauce, scallions, sesame oil, white pepper, and salt to the pot. Stir well to combine. Serve.

Nutritional Values:

- Calories: 98
- Net Carbs: 1g
- Fat: 6g
- Protein: 8g
- Sugar: 0g

Difficulty: 1 2 3 4 5

Cold Berry Mint Soup

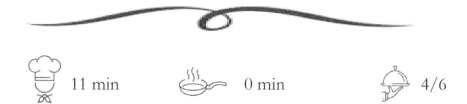

🧑‍🍳 11 min   🍳 0 min   🛎 4/6

Ingredients:

- two cups frozen mixed berries
- one cup unsweetened almond milk
- half cup fresh mint leaves, sliced
- quarter cup granulated erythritol sweetener
- 1 tsp lemon zest
- one tablespoon fresh lemon juice
- A tweak of salt

Directions:

1. Inside a blender, mix the berries, milk, mint leaves, sweetener, zest, lemon juice, and salt. Mix till uniform. Refrigerate for around 30 mins till chilled.
2. Pour the soup into serving containers or glasses and garnish with fresh mint leaves.

Nutritional Values:

- Calories: 110
- Net Carbs: 8g
- Fat: 6g
- Protein: 2g
- Sugar: 3g

Difficulty: **1** 2 3 4 5

Seafood Fish Stew

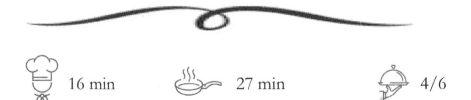

🍳 16 min   🍳 27 min   🍽 4/6

Ingredients:

- 1-pound white fish fillets, cut into chunks
- 8 oz shrimp, peeled and deveined
- 8 oz mussels or clams, cleaned
- 1/4 cup olive oil
- one onion, diced
- 3 cloves garlic, crushed
- quarter tsp red pepper flakes (optional)
- one red bell pepper, diced
- one zucchini, cut into half-moons
- two cups low-sodium seafood or vegetable broth
- two cups crushed tomatoes or tomato passata
- Salt & black pepper, as required
- Zest & juice of one lemon

Directions:

1. Warm the olive oil in your big pot across moderate flame. Include the onion, garlic, and red pepper flakes (if utilizing). Cook within 3-4 mins till softened and fragrant.
2. Include the red bell pepper and zucchini, then cook within five mins till vegetables are slightly tender.
3. Mix in the broth and crushed tomatoes. Top utilizing salt plus black pepper. Let it simmer and cook within five mins.
4. Include the fish chunks, and cook within five mins till the fish is almost cooked through.
5. Mix in the shrimp and mussels or clams. Cover and cook within five mins till seafood is cooked completely. Remove and stir in lemon zest and juice. Serve.

Nutritional Values:

- Calories: 350
- Net Carbs: 9g
- Fat: 18g
- Protein: 35g
- Sugar: 5g

Difficulty: 1 2 **3** 4 5

Fennel Pork Stew

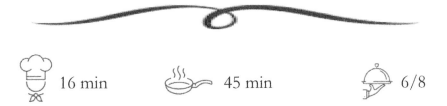

🧑‍🍳 16 min 🍳 45 min 🍽 6/8

Ingredients:

- two lbs. of pork shoulder, cubed
- 2 moderate fennel bulbs, thinly sliced
- one big onion, sliced
- 3 minced garlic cloves
- two cups low-sodium chicken broth
- 1/3 cup olive oil
- one tablespoon crushed fennel seeds
- Salt and pepper, as required

Directions:

1. Warm olive oil in your big pot across moderate-high flame.
2. Top the cubed pork utilizing salt plus pepper. Brown the pork within five mins. Afterwards, eliminate the cooked pork and put away.
3. In your same pot, include the onions and cook within five mins till softened and golden brown. Include the fennel and cook within five mins till it begins to soften.
4. Stir in the garlic and fennel seeds, then cook for another min.
5. Return the cooked pork and include the broth. Let it boil, adjust to low flame, conceal, and let it simmer within thirty mins or till the pork is softer. Regulate seasoning with salt plus pepper if required. Serve.

Nutritional Values:

- Calories: 420
- Net Carbs: 8g
- Fat: 30g
- Protein: 27g
- Sugar: 3g

Difficulty: 1 2 **3** 4 5

Curried Chicken Veg Stew

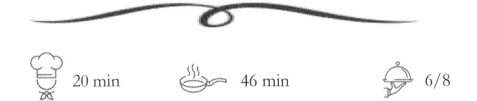

🍳 20 min   🍳 46 min   🍽 6/8

Ingredients:

- two lbs. boneless, skinless chicken breasts, cubed
- two tbsps. coconut oil
- one average onion, sliced
- two cloves garlic, crushed
- one tablespoon curry powder
- half teaspoon ground turmeric
- quarter teaspoon ground ginger
- quarter teaspoon cayenne pepper (optional)
- one cup chicken broth
- one (fourteen and a half ounces) can of diced tomatoes, drained
- two cups cauliflower florets
- one cup green beans, trimmed & halved
- 1 cup diced bell pepper
- Salt & black pepper, as required

Directions:

1. Warm your big pot with coconut oil across moderate flame. Include the onion and garlic, then cook within five mins till softened.
2. Stir in the curry powder, turmeric, ginger, and cayenne pepper (if utilized), and cook within one min to toast the spices. Include the chicken, then cook till browned on the entire ends.
3. Mix in the broth and tomatoes. Let it boil, adjust to low heat and simmer within twenty mins.
4. Include cauliflower, green beans, and bell pepper. Continue cooking within twenty mins till vegetables are softer. Regulate with salt and black pepper as needed. Serve.

Nutritional Values:

- Calories: 325
- Net Carbs: 6g
- Fat: 15g
- Protein: 36g
- Sugar: 4g

Difficulty: 1 **2** 3 4 5

Sausage Ratatouille Stew

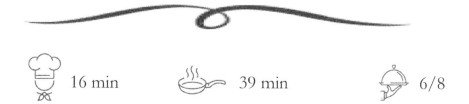

🧑‍🍳 16 min   🍳 39 min   🍽 6/8

Ingredients:

- one-lb. smoked sausage, sliced
- two moderate zucchinis, diced
- 1 moderate eggplant, diced
- 1 each of red & yellow bell pepper, diced
- one average onion, sliced
- three garlic cloves, crushed
- one (fourteen and a half oz.) can of diced tomatoes, no sugar included
- one cup low-sodium chicken broth
- two tbsp olive oil
- two tsp dried basil
- salt & pepper, as required

Directions:

1. Warm your big pot utilizing olive oil across moderate flame. Include the smoked sausage, then cook till browned. Eliminate the sausage and put away.
2. Include the onions and garlic to your same pot, then cook till fragrant. Include the zucchini, eggplant, and bell peppers. Cook for 5 mins, mixing regularly.
3. Mix in the tomatoes with juice, broth, dried basil, salt, and pepper. Return the cooked sausage to your pot and mix well.
4. Simmer within 30 mins till vegetables are tender. Serve hot.

Nutritional Values:

- Calories: 300
- Net Carbs: 9g
- Fat: 21g
- Protein: 17g
- Sugar: 6g

Difficulty: 1 2 **3** 4 5

Chapter 13: Salads, Snacks, and Sandwiches

Cold Broccoli Salad

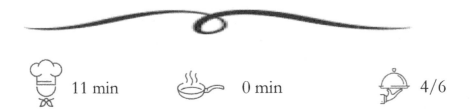

11 min   0 min   4/6

Ingredients:

- 4 cups broccoli florets, sliced into one-inch bite-size parts
- one cup shredded cheddar cheese
- ½ cup diced celery
- ½ cup sunflower seeds or roasted pumpkin seeds
- ¼ cup diced red onion
- ½ cup mayonnaise
- one tablespoon white wine vinegar
- one tablespoon granulated sugar-free sweetener, such as Swerve
- ½ tsp salt
- quarter teaspoon ground black pepper

Directions:

1. Combine the broccoli, cheddar cheese, celery, sunflower seeds, and red onion in your big container.
2. Toss simultaneously the mayonnaise, vinegar, sweetener, salt, and pepper in your small container. Drizzle the dressing across salad and whisk to cacross well. Serve.

Nutritional Values:

- Calories: 431
- Net Carbs: 5g
- Fat: 39g
- Protein: 13g
- Sugar: 3g

Difficulty: **1** 2 3 4 5

Kale Caesar Salad

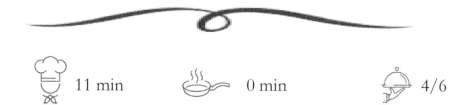

🧑‍🍳 11 min   🍳 0 min   🍽 4/6

Ingredients:

- one cup mayonnaise
- 2 small garlic cloves, pressed
- two tbsps. lemon juice
- one tbsp Dijon mustard
- two tsps. anchovy paste (optional)
- one teaspoon Worcestershire sauce
- ¼ teaspoon salt
- half teaspoon ground black pepper
- one big bunch of kale, inner stems removed & torn into bite-size pieces
- 4 oz shredded Parmesan cheese

Directions:

1. Mix the mayonnaise, garlic, lemon juice, mustard, anchovy paste, Worcestershire sauce, salt, and pepper in your small container.
2. Put the torn kale inside a big container with ½ cup of dressing and Parmesan cheese. Whisk to cover well and let sit for 20 mins up to one hr at ambient temp. to let the kale to soften. Serve.

Nutritional Values:

- Calories: 325
- Net Carbs: 2g
- Fat: 29g
- Protein: 12g
- Sugar: 0g

Difficulty: **1** 2 3 4 5

Cucumber Yogurt Salad

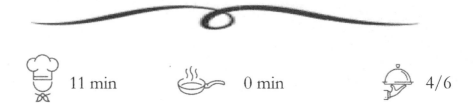

11 min   0 min   4/6

Ingredients:

- 1 cup whole-milk plain Greek yogurt
- quarter cup extra-virgin olive oil
- two tsp dried dill
- two garlic cloves, minced
- two tbsps. lemon juice
- 1 tsp salt
- ½ tsp ground black pepper
- 1 English cucumber, cut into half-moon slices
- ¼ red onion, thinly cut into half-moon slices

Directions:

1. Inside a small container, combine the yogurt, olive oil, dill, garlic, lemon juice, salt, and pepper, and toss till thoroughly combined and creamy.
2. Include the cucumber and onion slices and stir to mix. Serve.

Nutritional Values:

- Calories: 187
- Net Carbs: 5g
- Fat: 16g
- Protein: 6g
- Sugar: 0g

Difficulty: 1 2 3 4 5

Mixed Seed Crackers

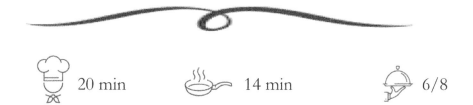

🎩 20 min   🍳 14 min   🍽 6/8

Ingredients:

- one cup almond flour
- one tbsp flaxseed
- one tbsp chia seed
- one tbsp cumin seed (optional)

- ½ teaspoon salt
- quarter teaspoon baking soda
- one big egg, beaten
- one tbsp extra-virgin olive oil

Directions:

1. Warm up the oven to 350°F.
2. Inside your big container, mix the almond flour, flaxseed, chia seed, cumin seed (if utilizing), salt, and baking soda.
3. Include the egg and olive oil to the dry ingredients and mix well till the dough forms a ball.
4. Put one layer of parchment paper on your countertop and place the dough ball on top. Cacross with a second layer of parchment and, utilizing your rolling pin, roll the dough to ⅛-inch thickness, aiming for a rectangular shape.
5. Remove the uppermost layer of parchment and, utilizing your pizza cutter, slice the dough into 1- to 2-inch-square crackers. Transfer the bottom layer of parchment with the cut cracker dough to a baking sheet.
6. Bake for twelve-fifteen mins, till the crackers are crispy and slightly golden. Allow cooling for 10 mins. Serve.

Nutritional Values:

- Calories: 159
- Net Carbs: 2g
- Fat: 14g
- Protein: 6g
- Sugar: 0g

Difficulty: 1 2 3 4 5

Cauliflower Nugget Bites

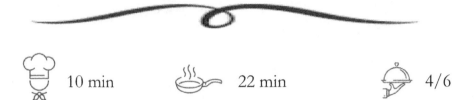

🍳 10 min   🍳 22 min   🍽 4/6

Ingredients:

- one big cauliflower head, sliced into bite-sized florets
- one cup almond flour
- half cup grated Parmesan cheese
- one teaspoon garlic powder
- half teaspoon onion powder
- half teaspoon paprika
- Salt & black pepper, as required
- 2 big eggs, beaten

Directions:

1. Preheat your oven to 400°F. Line a baking sheet utilizing parchment paper.
2. Mix the almond flour, Parmesan, garlic powder, onion powder, paprika, salt, and black pepper on a shallow plate.
3. Dip each cauliflower floret into the whisked eggs first, afterwards cacross it with the almond flour solution.
4. Put the coated cauliflower bites on the lined baking sheet. Bake within 20 mins till golden brown and crispy on the outside. Serve.

Nutritional Values:

- Calories: 275
- Net Carbs: 7g
- Fat: 19g
- Protein: 15g
- Sugar: 3g

Difficulty: 1 2 3 4 5

Easy Kale Chips

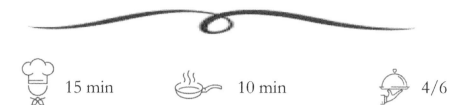

15 min   10 min   4/6

Ingredients:

- 1-pound fresh kale, trimmed & slice the leaves into bite-sized parts
- one tablespoon extra-virgin olive oil
- 1 tsp salt-free seasoning blend

Directions:

1. Warm up the oven to 350°F. Line a baking tray utilizing parchment paper.
2. Inside your big container, mix the kale, olive oil, and seasoning blend and toss till evenly coated.
3. Spread out the kale on your sheet pan and bake for ten mins or till crispy. Cool completely. Serve.

Nutritional Values:

- Calories: 58
- Net Carbs: 6g
- Fat: 3g
- Protein: 3g
- Sugar: 0g

Difficulty: **1** 2 3 4 5

Parmesan Cheese Crisps

🧑‍🍳 11 min   🍳 12 min   🛎 4/6

Ingredients:

- one cup grated Parmesan cheese
- half tsp each garlic powder & dried oregano
- 1/4 tsp black pepper

Directions:

1. Warm up the oven to 350°F. Line a baking sheet utilizing parchment paper.
2. Mix the Parmesan, garlic powder, oregano, and black pepper in your small container. Spoon tablespoons of the cheese mixture onto your baking sheet.
3. Flatten each mound of cheese utilizing the back of the spoon to form thin circles. Bake within 10 mins till the ends of the crisps are golden brown. Remove and cool it down. Serve.

Nutritional Values:

- Calories: 107
- Net Carbs: 1g
- Fat: 7g
- Protein: 9g
- Sugar: 0g

Difficulty: 1 2 3 4 5

Veggie and Hummus Sandwich

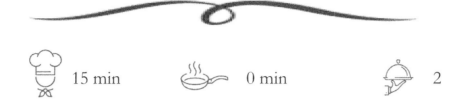

🍳 15 min   🍳 0 min   🍽 2

Ingredients:

- four pieces of low-carb bread
- half cup store-bought or homemade cauliflower hummus
- 1 small cucumber, thinly cut
- one moderate avocado, eroded, skinned and cut
- 2 cups mixed greens
- 6 cherry tomatoes, halved
- 1/4 cup alfalfa sprouts
- Salt & pepper, as required

Directions:

1. Disperse cauliflower hummus evenly on every bread piece. Layer the cucumber on two bread slices.
2. Top with the avocado slices, then season utilizing salt & pepper. Include a layer of mixed greens and cherry tomato halves.
3. Finish with a layer of alfalfa sprouts and cover with the rest of the bread pieces to form sandwiches. Serve.

Nutritional Values:

- Calories: 320
- Net Carbs: 11g
- Fat: 25g
- Protein: 17g
- Sugar: 5g

Difficulty: 1 2 3 4 5

Avocado Tomato Chicken Sandwich

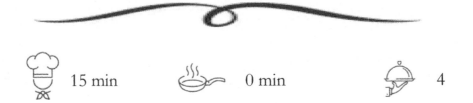

🍳 15 min   🍳 0 min   🍽 4

Ingredients:

- 8 slices of complete-grain, low-carb bread, toasted
- 1-pound boneless, skinless chicken breast, cooked & finely cut
- two avocados, ripe & finely cut
- two tomatoes, cut into rounds
- two cups mixed greens or lettuce leaves
- 4 tbsp sugar-free, light mayonnaise
- Salt & pepper to taste

Directions:

1. Spread 1 tbsp mayonnaise on every end of all bread slices. Layer chicken breast pieces evenly on the bottom piece of bread—season with salt plus pepper.
2. Include 1/4 of avocado slices, some tomato slices, and a layer of mixed greens. Top with another slice of bread. Repeat these steps for the remaining sandwiches. Serve.

Nutritional Values:

- Calories: 450
- Net Carbs: 12g
- Fat: 28g
- Protein: 35g
- Sugar: 2g

Difficulty: **1** 2 3 4 5

Tuna Salad English Muffin Sandwich

11 min   5 min   2

Ingredients:

- one (5 oz) tin tuna in water, drained
- 1/4 cup mayonnaise
- half small celery stalk, thinly sliced
- 1 tbsp red onion, thinly sliced
- half teaspoon Dijon mustard
- quarter teaspoon garlic powder
- Salt & black pepper, as required
- 2 low-carb English muffins, lightly toasted & cut in half
- 4 small lettuce leaves
- 2 tomato slices

Directions:

1. Combine the tuna, mayonnaise, celery, red onion, Dijon mustard, garlic powder, salt, and black pepper in your moderate container.
2. Place a lettuce leaf on each English muffin. Evenly distribute the tuna salad onto every lettuce leaf.
3. Season utilizing a tomato slice and another lettuce leaf. Close with the top halves of the English muffins.

Nutritional Values:

- Calories: 375
- Net Carbs: 5g
- Fat: 28g
- Protein: 24g
- Sugar: 2g

Difficulty: 1 2 3 4 5

Dried Fruit and Nut Bars

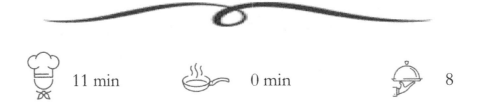

11 min   0 min   8

Ingredients:

- one cup each of unsalted almonds & walnuts
- quarter cup unsweetened coconut, ragged
- quarter cup each of sugar-free dried cranberries & dried apricots, chopped
- 2 tbsp chia seeds
- 2 tbsp flaxseeds, ground
- quarter cup smooth almond butter
- quarter cup coconut oil, melted

Directions:

1. Blend the almonds and walnuts in your mixing container till they are coarsely sliced. Include the coconut, cranberries, apricots, chia seeds, and ground flaxseeds and pulse to combine.
2. In your separate container, mix the almond butter and coconut oil. Put this solution into your food processor and pulse till evenly distributed.
3. Line your 8x8-inch baking pot utilizing parchment paper. Pour the mixture into your pot and press it firmly into an even layer.
4. Refrigerate the bars within 2 hours or overnight till they are firm. Cut them into eight equal pieces, then serve.

Nutritional Values:

- Calories: 320
- Net Carbs: 8g
- Fat: 28g
- Protein: 9g
- Sugar: 2g

Difficulty: **1** 2 3 4 5

Strawberry Yogurt Pops

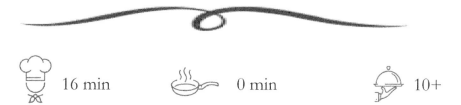

🍳 16 min   🍳 0 min   🍽 10+

Ingredients:

- 12 oz fresh or frozen (and thawed) strawberries, chopped
- ¼ cup + 2 tbsp granulated sugar-free sweetener, such as Swerve, divided
- 1½ cups full-fat plain Greek yogurt
- 2 tsp vanilla extract
- 1½ cups heavy (whipping) cream

Directions:

1. Combine the strawberries and ¼ cup of sweetener in your mixer and mix till pureed and smooth.
2. Transmit the mixture to your big container and whisk in the yogurt and vanilla extract.
3. Whip the cream with the remaining sweetener in another big container utilizing your electric blender till fluffy and stiff peaks are formed.
4. Warm the whipped cream into the yogurt-and-strawberry solution till well combined. Freeze in ice-pop molds and freeze within 6 to 8 hours till firm.

Nutritional Values:

- Calories: 166
- Net Carbs: 4g
- Fat: 14g
- Protein: 5g
- Sugar: 7g

Difficulty: 1 **2** 3 4 5

Peanut Butter Mousse

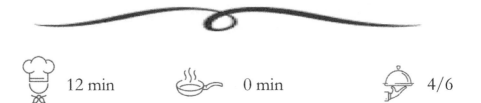

🧑‍🍳 12 min   🍳 0 min   🍽️ 4/6

Ingredients:

- 4 oz cream cheese at ambient temp.
- quarter cup natural peanut butter
- one cup heavy cream
- 3 tbsps. powdered sugar substitute

Directions:

1. Blend the cream cheese and peanut butter in your average container till they're well-mixed.
2. Combine the heavy cream and powdered sugar substitute in your moderate container. Use your hand blender on increased speed to whip till stiff peaks are formed.
3. Warm in the cream cheese and peanut butter mixture utilizing a spatula till no streaks remain. Put the mousse into serving dishes and serve.

Nutritional Values:

- Calories: 399
- Net Carbs: 5g
- Fat: 40g
- Protein: 6g
- Sugar: 9g

Difficulty: 1 **2** 3 4 5

Chocolate Mug Cake

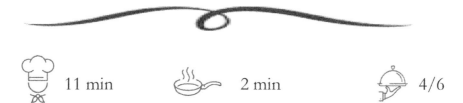

🍳 11 min   🍳 2 min   🍽 4/6

Ingredients:

- one tbsp salted butter
- ¼ cup superfine almond flour
- one big egg, beaten
- two tbsps. unsweetened cocoa powder
- two tbsps. sugar-free dark chocolate chips
- 2 tbsp granulated white sugar substitute
- ½ tsp baking powder

Directions:

1. Place the butter inside an oven-safe coffee mug and heat on high for 20 seconds or till melted.
2. Include the almond flour, beaten egg, cocoa powder, chocolate chips, sugar substitute, and baking powder, then mix well.
3. Cook the mug cake batter in the oven on high for 45 seconds, and check to see if it is set. Let the cake cool for 2 to 3 mins before enjoying it.

Nutritional Values:

- Calories: 84
- Net Carbs: 1g
- Fat: 7g
- Protein: 3g
- Sugar: 8g

Difficulty: 1 **2** 3 4 5

Pecan Sandie Cookies

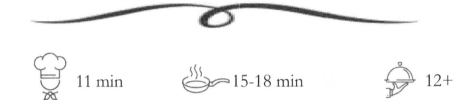

🧑‍🍳 11 min   🍳 15-18 min   🔔 12+

Ingredients:

- half cup (1 stick) unsalted butter, softened
- ½ cup granulated sugar-free sweetener, such as Swerve
- 1 big egg
- one teaspoon vanilla extract

- two cups almond flour
- one teaspoon xanthan gum
- ½ tsp baking powder
- half teaspoon ground cinnamon
- one cup sliced pecans

Directions:

1. The oven should be preheated to 350°F. Line a baking tray utilizing parchment paper.
2. Inside your big container, utilizing an electric blender on moderate speed, cream the butter and sweetener till smooth. Include the egg and vanilla and whisk thoroughly.
3. Include the almond flour, xanthan gum, baking powder, and cinnamon, and mix utilizing a wooden spatula till well incorporated. Mix in the pecans.
4. Spoon 2 tablespoon mounds of dough, around one inch separate, on your baking tray.
5. Bake the cookies within 15 to 18 mins, till set and lightly golden. Let sit on the baking sheet for ten mins prior to transmitting it to your cooling rack.

Nutritional Values:

- Calories: 246
- Net Carbs: 2g
- Fat: 24g
- Protein: 5g
- Sugar: 8g

Difficulty: 1 **2** 3 4 5

Cheesecake Raspberries Fluff

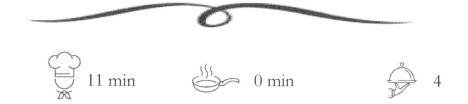

🧑‍🍳 11 min   🍳 0 min   🍽️ 4

Ingredients:

- two-third cup heavy cream
- 6 ounces cream cheese at ambient temp.
- one-third cup powdered sugar substitute
- ¼ teaspoon pure vanilla extract
- ½ cup raspberries
- ¼ cup slivered toasted almonds

Directions:

1. Inside an average container, whip the cream with a hand blender on high speed till stiff peaks form, about 4 mins. Set it aside.
2. Use the hand mixer inside a second moderate container to whip the cream cheese, sugar substitute, and vanilla extract on high speed till light and fluffy.
3. Wrap the whipped cream into your cream cheese solution utilizing a spatula till well combined. Split the mixture among 4 serving dishes, and season with the raspberries and almonds.

Nutritional Values:

- Calories: 325
- Net Carbs: 4g
- Fat: 32g
- Protein: 5g
- Sugar: 10g

Difficulty: 1 2 **3** 4 5

Avocado Chocolate Mousse

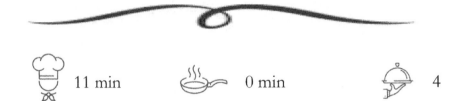

11 min   0 min   4

Ingredients:

- 2 ripe avocados, eroded & peeled
- ¼ cup unsweetened cocoa powder
- quarter cup heavy (whipping) cream, + extra as needed
- 2 to 4 tbsp granulated sugar-free sweetener, such as Swerve (optional)
- 2 tsps. vanilla extract
- half teaspoon cinnamon (optional)
- ¼ tsp salt

Directions:

1. In a blender, combine the avocados, cocoa powder, heavy cream, sweetener (if utilizing), vanilla, cinnamon (if utilizing), and salt, and blend till smooth and creamy.
2. If the mixture is too dense, include cream one tbsp. at a time. Serve immediately.

Nutritional Values:

- Calories: 183
- Net Carbs: 3g
- Fat: 17g
- Protein: 3g
- Sugar: 0g

Difficulty: 1 2 3 4 5

Frozen Fruit Sorbet

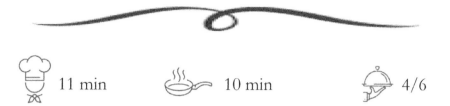

🍳 11 min   🍳 10 min   🛎 4/6

Ingredients:

- 8 oz chopped ripe fruit of choice
- 1 tbsp Truvia sweetener
- 3 tbsp water

Directions:

1. Put the fruit in one layer on a sheet pan and freeze within 2 hours till frozen.
2. Meanwhile, in your small saucepan across moderate flame, combine the Truvia and water and cook within two to three mins, stirring, till the sweetener dissolves.
3. Simmer within 5 mins till it thickens into syrup. Set aside.
4. Place the frozen fruit inside a mixing container and pulse to crush the fruit. With the motor running, include the syrup and purée till smooth. Serve.

Nutritional Values:

- Calories: 183
- Net Carbs: 3g
- Fat: 17g
- Protein: 3g
- Sugar: 0g

Difficulty: 1 2 **3** 4 5

Mini Strawberry Cheesecakes

🧑‍🍳 11 min   🍳 16 min   🍽 6/8

Ingredients:

- one (8-oz) block of cream cheese, softened
- quarter cup granulated white sugar substitute
- one big egg
- 1 tbsp sour cream
- ¼ tsp pure vanilla extract
- ½ cup sliced fresh strawberries

Directions:

1. Preheat the oven to 350°F—line 6 cups of a regular-size muffin tin utilizing parchment paper muffin liners.
2. Place the cream cheese inside a moderate container and include the sugar substitute. Utilizing a hand blender, whisk the sugar and cream cheese on high till the solution is light and fluffy.
3. Include the egg, sour cream, and vanilla, and continue mixing till thoroughly combined. Divide the mixture among the 6 muffin tins. Bake within 15 mins or till the cheesecakes are set.
4. Cool it down. When cool, top each with a few strawberry slices and serve.

Nutritional Values:

- Calories: 150
- Net Carbs: 3g
- Fat: 14g
- Protein: 3g
- Sugar: 10g

Difficulty: 1 2 **3** 4 5

Peanut Butter Energy Balls

🧑‍🍳 22 min   🍳 0 min   🍽️ 12 energy balls

Ingredients:

- one cup unsweetened peanut or almond butter, stirred well
- ½ cup almond or coconut flour
- ¼ cup rolled quick-cooking oats
- 2 to 4 tbsp granulated sugar-free sweetener (optional)
- ¼ cup unsweetened coconut flakes
- ¼ cup sugar-free chocolate chips, chopped, such as Lily's
- 2 tbsp chia seeds

Directions:

1. Inside your big container, mix the peanut butter, almond flour, oats, sweetener (if utilizing), coconut flakes, chocolate chips, and chia seeds.
2. Utilizing your hands, form the solution into 12 balls, about 1 ½ inch in diameter each.
3. Transfer the energy balls to an airtight storage container, with a piece of parchment paper among each layer. Keep in your refrigerator till firm. Serve.

Nutritional Values:

- Calories: 203
- Net Carbs: 6g
- Fat: 17g
- Protein: 7g
- Sugar: 1g

Difficulty: 1 **2** 3 4 5

Chocolate Nut Clusters

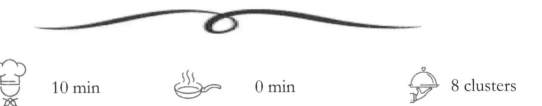

🍳 10 min   🍳 0 min   🍽 8 clusters

Ingredients:

- quarter cup sugar-free dark choco chips (such as Lily's)
- ½ tsp coconut oil
- ¾ cup mixed nuts

Directions:

1. Combine the dark choco chips and coconut oil inside a moderate oven-safe container. Warm for thirty seconds on high, stir and repeat till the chocolate chips are dissolved.
2. Include the nuts and combine till they're all coated. Scoop out a spoonful of mixture and drop it onto your parchment paper–lined baking sheet.
3. Refrigerate the clusters for at least 1 hour to let them set. Serve.

Nutritional Values:

- Calories: 205
- Net Carbs: 4g
- Fat: 17g
- Protein: 3g
- Sugar: 2g

Difficulty: 1 **2** 3 4 5

Pineapple-Peanut Nice Cream

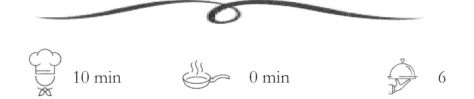

🧑‍🍳 10 min   🍳 0 min   🍽️ 6

Ingredients:

- two cups frozen pineapple
- one cup no added sugar peanut butter
- ½ cup unsweetened almond milk

Directions:

1. Inside your mixer or mixing container, mix the frozen pineapple and peanut butter and process.
2. Include the almond milk, then blend till smooth. Serve.

Nutritional Values:

- Calories: 301
- Net Carbs: 8g
- Fat: 22g
- Protein: 14g
- Sugar: 8g

Difficulty: **1** 2 3 4 5

Watermelon Fruit Pizza

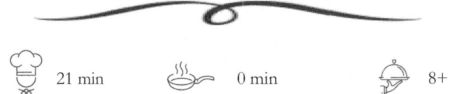

🧑‍🍳 21 min   🍳 0 min   🍽 8+

Ingredients:

- one moderate seedless watermelon
- one cup unsweetened coconut cream
- one teaspoon vanilla extract
- two tbsps. erythritol
- half cup unsweetened shredded coconut
- half cup sliced almonds
- quarter cup unsweetened cocoa nibs or sugar-free chocolate chips
- half cup fresh berries

Directions:

1. Cut a slice of watermelon about 1 inch thick to form the pizza base.
2. Inside a moderate container, mix coconut cream, vanilla, and erythritol. Combine thoroughly to form a smooth. Disperse the coconut cream solution evenly across the watermelon slice.
3. Drizzle shredded coconut across the coconut cream layer. Top with almonds, cocoa nibs, and fresh berries. Slice the watermelon fruit pizza into eight equal pieces and serve.

Nutritional Values:

- Calories: 190
- Net Carbs: 4g
- Fat: 14g
- Protein: 4g
- Sugar: 6g

Difficulty: 1 **2** 3 4 5

Raspberry-Chocolate Chia Pudding

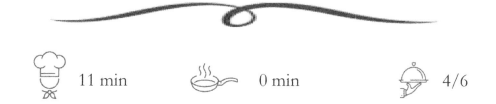

🧑‍🍳 11 min   🍳 0 min   🍽 4/6

Ingredients:

- half cup raspberries, fresh or frozen (thawed)
- 1 cup almond milk (unsweetened)
- 1 cup full-fat tinned unsweetened coconut milk
- 2 to 4 tbsp granulated sugar-free sweetener (optional)
- ½ cup chia seeds
- ¼ cup no-sugar-added chocolate protein powder

Directions:

1. Put the raspberries inside a big container and beat them thoroughly utilizing a fork. Include the almond milk, coconut milk, and sweetener t (if utilizing), and toss till uniform.
2. Include the chia seeds and protein powder, and toss till well mixed. Divide the mixture evenly among 4 ramekins or small jars. Cover and refrigerate within 6 hours before serving cold.

Nutritional Values:

- Calories: 247
- Net Carbs: 6g
- Fat: 18g
- Protein: 11g
- Sugar: 0g

Difficulty: 1 **2** 3 4 5

Orange and Peach Ambrosia

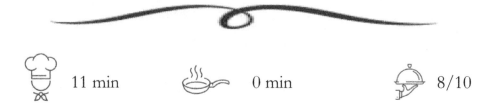

🍳 11 min   🍳 0 min   🍽 8/10

Ingredients:

- 3 oranges, peeled, sectioned, & quartered
- 2 (4- oz) cups diced peaches in water, drained
- 1 cup shredded, unsweetened coconut
- 1 (8-oz) container fat-free crème fraîche

Directions:

1. Inside a big mixing container, mix the oranges, peaches, coconut, and crème fraîche.
2. Gently toss till well mixed. Cover and refrigerate overnight. Serve.

Nutritional Values:

- Calories: 111
- Net Carbs: 5g
- Fat: 5g
- Protein: 2g
- Sugar: 8g

Difficulty: **1** 2 3 4 5

Chapter 15: Sauces, Dressings, and Toppings

Tzatziki Sauce

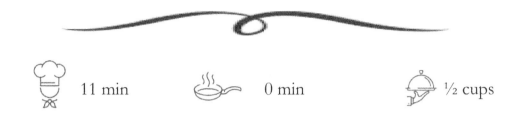

11 min   0 min   ½ cups

Ingredients:

- one cup low-fat plain Greek yogurt
- ½ English cucumber, grated, with all the liquid squeezed out
- Juice of ½ lemon
- one tablespoon sliced fresh dill
- one teaspoon crushed garlic
- Sea salt & ground black pepper, as required

Directions:

1. Inside your small container, stir together the yogurt, cucumber, dill, lemon juice, and garlic till well blended—top utilizing salt and pepper.
2. Refrigerate the sauce inside an airtight container for around 5 days.

Nutritional Values:

- Calories: 31
- Net Carbs: 4g
- Fat: 1g
- Protein: 2g
- Sugar: 3g

Difficulty: **1** 2 3 4 5

Avocado Spread

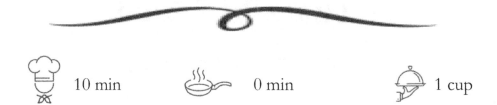

🧑‍🍳 10 min   🍳 0 min   🍽 1 cup

Ingredients:

- one big avocado, halved, eroded, and skinned
- Juice of ½ lime
- one teaspoon extra-virgin olive oil
- half teaspoon black pepper
- ¼ cup sliced fresh cilantro

Directions:

1. Place the avocado inside a blender or moderate container, blend it, or mash it with a fork.
2. Include the lime juice, olive oil, black pepper, and cilantro and blend or stir vigorously till combined.
3. Stock the spread in a Vacuum-packed container in the fridge for around five days.

Nutritional Values:

- Calories: 181
- Net Carbs: 3g
- Fat: 16g
- Protein: 2g
- Sugar: 1g

Difficulty: **1** 2 3 4 5

Herbed Yogurt Sauce

🍳 10 min   🍳 0 min   🍽 1 ½ cup

Ingredients:

- half cup Italian parsley leaves
- one garlic clove
- 1 cup full-fat plain Greek yogurt
- ¼ cup extra-virgin olive oil
- quarter cup lemon juice
- one tsp salt
- ¼ tsp ground black pepper

Directions:

1. Mix the parsley and garlic inside a blender and blend till well chopped.
2. Include the yogurt, olive oil, pepper, salt and lemon juice and pulse till uniform. Keep in your sealed container in fridge for up to 1 week.

Nutritional Values:

- Calories: 117
- Net Carbs: 2g
- Fat: 11g
- Protein: 4g
- Sugar: 0g

Difficulty: **1** 2 3 4 5

Smoky Barbecue Sauce

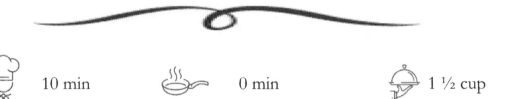

🍳 10 min   🍳 0 min   🍽 1 ½ cup

Ingredients:

- one (15-oz) can of no-salt-added crushed tomatoes
- 2 tbsp no-salt-included tomato paste
- two tbsp apple cider vinegar
- 1 tbsp smoked paprika
- two tsps. garlic powder
- one teaspoon onion powder
- tweak ground cayenne pepper

Directions:

1. Put the tomatoes, tomato paste, vinegar, paprika, garlic powder, onion powder, and cayenne inside an average pot across moderate-low flame.
2. Let it simmer, adjust to low flame, and simmer for 10 mins. Allow the sauce to cool and keep in the fridge in an airtight bowl for up to 1 week.

Nutritional Values:

- Calories: 28
- Net Carbs: 6g
- Fat: 0g
- Protein: 1g
- Sugar: 3g

Difficulty: 1 2 3 4 5

Ranch Dressing

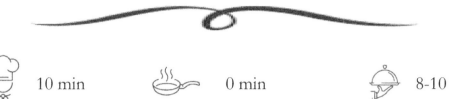

🧑‍🍳 10 min   🍳 0 min   🍽 8-10

Ingredients:

- 8 oz fat-free plain Greek yogurt
- quarter cup low-fat buttermilk
- one tablespoon garlic powder
- one tablespoon dried dill
- one tbsp dried chives
- one tablespoon onion powder
- one tablespoon dried parsley
- Pinch ground black pepper

Directions:

1. Inside a shallow, moderate container, mix the Greek yogurt & buttermilk.
2. Stir in the garlic powder, dill, chives, onion powder, parsley, and pepper. Serve with a vegetable stick of your choice.

Nutritional Values:

- Calories: 29
- Net Carbs: 3g
- Fat: 0g
- Protein: 3g
- Sugar: 2g

Difficulty: 1 2 3 4 5

Green Goddess Dressing

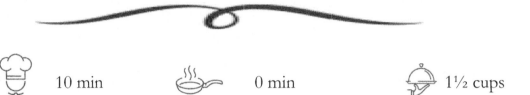

🧑‍🍳 10 min   🍳 0 min   🍽 1½ cups

Ingredients:

- two very ripe avocados, pitted and peeled
- ½ cup packed cilantro or parsley leaves
- ½ cup mayonnaise
- Zest of one lemon
- Juice of one lemon
- one teaspoon garlic powder
- one tbsp dried chives
- one teaspoon salt
- quarter teaspoon ground black pepper
- Warm water, as required

Directions:

1. In a mixer, blend the avocados, cilantro, mayonnaise, lemon zest and juice, garlic powder, dried chives, salt, and pepper till smooth.
2. Include warm water, 1 spoon at a time, mixing after each addition till the desired consistency. Serve.

Nutritional Values:

- Calories: 102
- Net Carbs: 1g
- Fat: 10g
- Protein: 1g
- Sugar: 0g

Difficulty: 1 2 3 4 5

Whipped Cream Topping

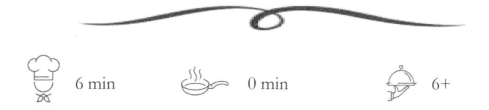

🧑‍🍳 6 min   🍳 0 min   🛎 6+

Ingredients:

- one cup heavy cream, cold
- quarter cup powdered erythritol (a sugar substitute)
- one teaspoon vanilla extract

Directions:

1. Inside a mixing container, mix the cold heavy cream and powdered erythritol. Utilizing your hand mixer, mix on low speed till the erythritol is incorporated into the cream.
2. Elevate the speed to moderate-high and start to whisk till soft peaks are set. Include vanilla extract and continue to whisk till rigid peaks are formed. Serve immediately or store in the refrigerator.

Nutritional Values:

- Calories: 164
- Net Carbs: 2g
- Fat: 17g
- Protein: 1g
- Sugar: 0g

Difficulty: 1 2 3 4 5

Chocolate Frosting

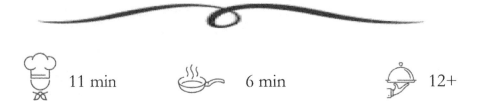

🧑‍🍳 11 min   🍳 6 min   🍽 12+

Ingredients:

- two cups powdered erythritol
- half cup unsweetened cocoa powder
- quarter cup unsalted butter, softened
- quarter cup unsweetened almond milk
- two tsps. vanilla extract

Directions:

1. Inside a moderate container, mix the erythritol and cocoa powder.
2. In another container, cream the softened butter utilizing a hand mixer on moderate speed within 1 min.
3. Gradually include the erythritol and cocoa powder mixture, continuing to mix till well combined. Slowly pour the milk and vanilla while mixing on low speed till fully incorporated.
4. Once all ingredients are well combined and smooth, set aside a few mins to firm up slightly. Apply the frosting to your desired cake or dessert.

Nutritional Values:

- Calories: 60
- Net Carbs: 1g
- Fat: 5g
- Protein: 1g
- Sugar: 0g

Difficulty: **1** 2 3 4 5

Butterscotch Topping

🧑‍🍳 16 min   🍳 22 min   🍽️ 4/6

Ingredients:

- half cup unsalted butter
- half cup erythritol
- one cup heavy cream
- one teaspoon pure vanilla extract
- quarter teaspoon salt
- quarter teaspoon xanthan gum

Directions:

1. In your moderate pot, dissolve the butter across low flame. Include the erythritol and stir till well combined.
2. Gradually pour the heavy cream while stirring continuously. Adjust to moderate heat and continue stirring till the solution begins to bubble.
3. Include the vanilla and salt, and stir to combine. Cook for another 8-10 mins, occasionally stirring, till it thickens slightly.
4. Whisk in the xanthan gum and cook within 1-2 mins till the butterscotch reaches a thick, glossy consistency.
5. Remove and let it cool for a few mins before utilizing it in your desired dessert.

Nutritional Values:

- Calories: 190
- Net Carbs: 6g
- Fat: 18g
- Protein: 1g
- Sugar: 0g

Difficulty: **1** 2 3 4 5

30-DAY MEAL PLAN

DAY	BREAKFAST	LUNCH	DINNER	DESSERTS
1	Breakfast Spinach Shakshuka	Mushroom Chili Stroganoff	Chimichurri Tuna Steaks	Dried Fruit and Nut Bars
2	Pesto Egg And Ham Roll-Ups	Pan-Fried Cod with Slaw	Chicken Broccoli Alfredo	Orange And Peach Ambrosia
3	Breakfast Potato Zucchini Hash	Cauliflower Rice Tabbouleh	Zoodles with Beef Meatballs	Raspberry-Chocolate Chia Pudding
4	Eggs Stuffed Avocado Boats	Cold Berry Mint Soup	Clam Cauliflower Chowder	Watermelon Fruit Pizza
5	Corned Beef Hash	Tempeh and Veggie Curry	Lean Turkey Meatballs	Pineapple-Peanut Nice Cream
6	Sausage and Cheese Egg Muffins	Seared Scallops with Spring Vegetables	Lime Lamb Cutlets	Chocolate Nut Clusters
7	Berry Walnut Yogurt Parfait	Portobello Kung Pao	Garlic Butter Shrimp with Vegetables	Pecan Sandie Cookies
8	Almond Butter Pancakes	Egg Drop Soup	One-Pot Chicken Margherita	Peanut Butter Energy Balls
9	Poppyseed Lemon Muffins	Zucchini Au Gratin	Herbed Lamb Chops	Mini Strawberry Cheesecakes
10	Whipped Cottage Cheese Breakfast Container	Roasted Carrot Leek Soup	Mediterranean Poached Tuna	Frozen Fruit Sorbet
11	Baked N'oatmeal with Berries	Garlic Tempeh Lettuce Wraps	Coconut-Curry Chicken	Avocado Chocolate Mousse
12	Blueberry French Toast	Garlic Butter Chicken with Cauliflower Rice	Pork Chops with Creamy Mushroom Sauce	Cheesecake Raspberries Fluff
13	Apple Cinnamon Scones	Cabbage Skillet with Kielbasa	Fish Cakes with Garlic Sauce	Strawberry Yogurt Pops
14	Avocado Toast with Fried Egg	California Burger Wraps	One-Pan Lemon Herbed Chicken	Chocolate Mug Cake
15	Strawberry-Mint Baked Ricotta	Eggplant Parm in Sheet-Pan	Flank Steak with Creamy Pepper Sauce	Peanut Butter Mousse

16	Breakfast Spinach Shakshuka	Garlicky Mushroom Soup	Salmon with Asparagus in Sheet Pan	Dried Fruit and Nut Bars
17	Pesto Egg And Ham Roll-Ups	Three Cheeses Stuffed Bell Peppers	Curried Chicken Vegetable Stew	Orange And Peach Ambrosia
18	Breakfast Potato Zucchini Hash	Ground Turkey Lettuce Wraps	Baked Bratwurst with Sauerkraut	Raspberry-Chocolate Chia Pudding
19	Eggs Stuffed Avocado Boats	Cold Broccoli Salad	Citrus Glazed Trout	Watermelon Fruit Pizza
20	Corned Beef Hash	Lamb Peppers Lettuce Cups	Fennel Pork Stew	Pineapple-Peanut Nice Cream
21	Sausage and Cheese Egg Muffins	Tuna Salad English Muffin Sandwich	Spinach Goat Cheese Stuffed Pork Loin	Chocolate Nut Clusters
22	Berry Walnut Yogurt Parfait	Creamy Tomato and Basil Soup	Coconut-Curry Shrimp	Pecan Sandie Cookies
23	Almond Butter Pancakes	Turkey Enchilada Container	Chimichurri Tuna Steaks	Peanut Butter Energy Balls
24	Poppyseed Lemon Muffins	Avocado Tomato Chicken Sandwich	Seafood Fish Stew	Mini Strawberry Cheesecakes
25	Whipped Cottage Cheese Breakfast Container	Orange Tofu with Broccoli	Chicken Cordon Bleu Casserole	Frozen Fruit Sorbet
26	Baked N'oatmeal with Berries	Kale Caesar Salad	Chicken Broccoli Alfredo	Avocado Chocolate Mousse
27	Blueberry French Toast	Veggie & Hummus Sandwich	Zoodles with Beef Meatballs	Cheesecake Raspberries Fluff
28	Apple Cinnamon Scones	Avocado Broccoli Soup	Sweet and Sour Turkey	Strawberry Yogurt Pops
29	Avocado Toast with Fried Egg	Pork and Green Bean Stir-Fry	Clam Cauliflower Chowder	Chocolate Mug Cake
30	Strawberry-Mint Baked Ricotta	Cucumber Yogurt Salad	Sausage Ratatouille Stew	Peanut Butter Mousse

COOKING CONVERSION CHART

Volume Equivalents (Liquid)

US STANDARD	US STANDARD (OUNCES)	METRIC (APPROXIMATE)
2 tablespoons	1 fl. oz.	30 mL
¼ cup	2 fl. oz.	60 mL
½ cup	4 fl. oz.	120 mL
1 cup	8 fl. oz.	240 mL
1½ cups	12 fl. oz.	355 mL
2 cups or 1 pint	16 fl. oz.	475 mL
4 cups or 1 quart	32 fl. oz.	1 L
1 gallon	128 fl. oz.	4 L

Volume Equivalents (Dry)

US STANDARD	METRIC (APPROXIMATE)
⅛ teaspoon	0.5 mL
¼ teaspoon	1 mL
½ teaspoon	2 mL
¾ teaspoon	4 mL
1 teaspoon	5 mL
1 tablespoon	15 mL
¼ cup	59 mL
⅓ cup	79 mL
½ cup	118 mL
⅔ cup	156 mL
¾ cup	177 mL
1 cup	235 mL
2 cups or 1 pint	475 mL
3 cups	700 mL
4 cups or 1 quart	1 L
½ gallon	2 L
1 gallon	4 L

Oven Temperatures

FAHRENHEIT (F)	CELSIUS (C) (APPROXIMATE)
250	120
300	150
325	165
350	180
375	190
400	200
425	220
450	230

Weight Equivalents

US STANDARD	METRIC (APPROXIMATE)
½ ounce	15 g
1 ounce	30 g
2 ounces	60 g
4 ounces	115 g
8 ounces	225 g
12 ounces	340 g
16 ounces or 1 pound	455 g

Conclusion

The journey toward managing diabetes and adopting a healthier lifestyle can be challenging. Still, this book has shown that enjoying delicious and satisfying meals is possible while maintaining balanced blood sugar levels. This cookbook has equipped you with extensive recipes and a comprehensive meal plan to help you transition smoothly into a diabetic-friendly diet.

Across the course of 1500 days, you have explored a wide variety of mouthwatering recipes that cater to every meal of the day. From breakfast containers to nutritious salads, hearty main courses, and guilt-free desserts - this cookbook has provided diabetic-friendly options for all your culinary needs. The 30-day meal plan included in the book acts as an invaluable guide to kickstart your journey toward better health and wellness.

As you continue to embrace this new way of eating and living, remember that consistency is key. It's essential to stay committed to your dietary restrictions and monitor your blood sugar levels regularly. By doing so, you are not only taking control of your diabetes but also improving your overall quality of life.

We hope this cookbook has helped debunk the myth that diabetic diets are limited or bland. In fact, the diverse array of meals presented in this book demonstrates that there's no shortage of delectable flavors when creating dishes suitable for diabetics. Use these recipes as an inspiration and explore new ways to incorporate diabetic-friendly ingredients into your cooking repertoire.

As you embark on your journey towards improved health, remember the importance of self-care and support from loved ones. Nurturing your physical health is only one aspect; emotional well-being is equally crucial in managing diabetes effectively.

Let *"DIABETIC DIET AFTER 50"* be more than just a cookbook; let it be a constant reminder that living with diabetes does not mean sacrificing great taste and variety in your meals. Enjoy the recipes, embrace the lifestyle, and embark on a healthier, happier journey towards better management of your diabetes.

Obtain your journal NOW! Scan the QR code below:

Made in the USA
Las Vegas, NV
09 September 2023